TOURISM Hotel English Conversation

영화로 보는
관광·호텔영어

최창현 · 임선희 공저

백산출판사

Preface

영어는 학문하기 위한 도구이기도 하지만 전 세계를 무대로 활동하기 위한 도구이기도 하다. 필자의 경우 대학에서 영어원서로 공부할 기회는 학과에서 개설한 원서강독한 과목뿐이라 영문과의 20세기 영미소설, 18세기 영미소설, 정외과에서 개설한 국제정치론, 사회학과의 사회변동론, 그리고 산업심리학과의 동기이론 등 6과목을 원서로 수업하는 과목을 수강하였다. 이는 인생에서 매우 중요한 밑거름이 되었다.

또 하나 인생에서 매우 중요한 밑거름이 된 계기는 1973년 봄으로, 당시 종로 2가에 위치한 EMI 영어학원에서 새벽 단과반을 수강했었다. 나는 중 2였고 수강생들은 대부분 마지막 입시를 목전에 둔 중 3이었다. 교재는 안현필 영어 실력 기초였던 걸로 기억한다.

첫날 가보니 한 150여 명 들어가는 강의실에 뒤는 자리가 없고 여학생만 혼자 앉아있는 앞자리가 한두 줄 비어 있어 선생님이 앞으로 오라고 하셨다. 처음에는 왜 앞줄이 비어 있는지 몰랐다. 선생님은 수업시간마다 암기할 문장이 20여 개 적혀 있는 8절지 종이를 나눠주시고 다음 날 물어보시니 그 여학생을 빼고는 모두 앞자리를 피했던 것이었다.

머리를 단아하게 묶은 그 여학생은 사춘기의 나에게는 연상의 여인이었다. 연상의 여인을 두고 자존심 상하게 뒷자리로 가기 싫어 기초 문법도 모르는 채 무조건 하루에 20여 개의 문장을 외웠다. 저녁에 암기하고도 불안해 엄마더러 새벽에 깨워달래서 목욕재계 후 상쾌한 마음으로 다시 암기했다.

시간이 흘러 한 달이 다 되자 선생님이 아직 중 2이니 한 달 더 들어보라고 하셔서

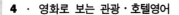
다음 한 달을 또 등록했다. 기대한 대로 그 연상의 여학생도 앞줄에 앉아 있었다. 어찌나 기쁜지 또 미친 듯이 500여 개의 문장을 외우니 문법이 저절로 이해되기 시작했다.

이 수업 덕분에 아마 내가 수입부에서 업무를 원활히 처리하고, 유학도 가고, 10여 년 전 파고다 외국어학원에서 토익강의할 기회도 얻고, 이를 계기로 현재 재직 중인 대학의 학과에 공무원 영어과목을 개설하고 토익 책을 집필해 학생들에게 공무원 시험의 당락을 결정짓는 영어를 가르칠 수 있게 되었고 이번에는 관광영어를 영어로 출간하게 되었으니 무척 행복하다.

위의 필자와는 달리 관광산업체인 호텔의 현장경험을 통해 영어를 익히고 공부한 필자는 15년여의 현장 일을 매우 즐겼다는 것이 솔직한 심정이다. 가끔 3교대를 했던 시간이 힘들기도 했지만 돌이켜보면 그로 인해 부지런해지고 밤낮으로 시간을 활용할 수 있어 일어와 중국어도 배우러 다니고 야학의 자원봉사교사로서 영어를 가르칠 수 있었기 때문이다. 각국에서 온 관광객들에게서 새롭고 앞선 정보를 접하고, 다양하고 개성 있는 패션감각을 익혔다. 고품격 호텔문화에 대한 자연스런 인지는 덤으로 체화되는 행운이었다.

100년의 역사와 전통을 자랑하는 영국의 호텔 레스토랑에서 수백 명을 대상으로 한 행사를 마치면 호텔에서 제공하는 온갖 음식을 맘대로 먹을 수 있었고 일류 주방장의 소스를 곁들인 따뜻한 램 스테이크를 맛볼 수 있었는데 그 맛은 지금도 잊을 수가 없다. 그 무엇보다도 8시간 근무하는 내내 클래식 BGM이 흐르는 환경에서 일할 수 있는 직군이 얼마나 될까 싶다.

매일 최소 15분 이상 이 교재를 통해 하루 열두 번 상대방을 칭찬하는 일에 열을 올리는 외국인들에게 여러분의 백만 불짜리 미소를 보여줄 것을 기대한다.

이 책은 첫째, TOEIC 강의와 TOEIC 책 저술의 경험을 바탕으로 쉬운 어휘와 문법 위주로 관광영어를 집필하려 했다. 둘째, 각 장 뒤에 Quiz 문제와 Vocabulary 등을 넣어 학생들이 관광영어를 자연스럽게 습득하도록 했다. 셋째, 이해를 돕기 위해 다양한 그림과 표 등을 많이 사용하려고 노력한 것이 특징이다. 모쪼록 이 책이 관광·호텔 관련 영어를 공부하려는 분들에게 많은 도움이 되기를 바란다.

2016년 10월

저자 일동

Contents

PART 2
호텔영어(English for Hotel Staff)

PART

1 관광영어
(English for Tourism)

Chapter 1

이탈리아 공항에서
(At the Airport in Italy)

- 영화 '로마의 휴일(Holiday in Rome)' 관광

1. 대화(Target Language)

　많은 사람들이 첫 해외여행의 경우 목적지 공항에 도착하여 입국심사를 위해 여권 (Passport)을 손에 꼭 쥐고 줄지어 기다리는 동안 약간의 긴장감과 묘한 떨림을 경험했을 것이다. 입국심사원이 하는 질문은 대체로 '출신국가가 어딘지, 입국의 목적이 무엇인지, 어디서 머물 것인가?' 이 세 가지 범주를 벗어나지 않는다. 가끔 너무 긴장하여 심사원의 질문에 엉뚱한 답을 하는 경우도 있으니 충분한 연습으로 여행지로의 입국을 즐겨보자.

A : Welcome to Rome. May I see your passport please?

B : Sure. Here it is.

A : Where are you coming from?

B : I'm coming from Seoul, Korea.

A : What is the purpose of your visit?

B : I'm here on business. (or I'm on a holiday : 휴가를 보내러 왔다. 여행)

A : How long are you planning to stay?

B : I'll be staying for three weeks.

A : Where will you be staying?

B : I'll be staying at a hotel.

A : Have you ever been to Rome before?

B : No, this is my first time.

A : Do you have anything to declare?

B : No, nothing particular.

A : Enjoy your stay.

B : Thank you.

🎞 영화 '로마의 휴일'(Holiday in Rome) 관광

로마의 휴일은 1953년 유럽의 어느 나라 공주가 유럽순방 마지막 나라로 이탈리아 로마에 온다는 설정으로 만들어진 영화다. 앤 공주(오드리 헵번)는 왕실의 제약과 정해진 스케줄에 싫증이 나자 로마를 여행하던 중 왕실을 몰래 빠져 나간다. 앤은 길거

리에서 잠이 들었고 한 신사의 도움으로 서민의 생활을 즐긴다.

그러나 그 신사는 특종을 찾아다니는 신문기자였다. 처음에는 단지 특종을 잡기 위해서 앤 공주와 로마의 거리를 다니며 공주가 한번도 해보지 못한 일들을 하며 여러 가지 해프닝을 벌인다. 이 모든 것이 그에게는 큰 특종이다. 이 사실을 모른 채 앤 공주는 친절한 그에게 정이 들었고 단지 특종만을 위해서 그녀와 함께했던 기자 조(그레고리 펙) 역시 순수한 앤 공주에게 끌리기 시작한다.

드디어 앤은 궁전으로 다시 돌아갔고 조가 신문기자였던 것을 알게 된 앤은 그에게 실망한다. 그러나 조는 앤 공주의 사진을 기사로 쓰지 않고 그녀에게 선물이라며 전해준다.

Asking for Directions

Could you tell me how to get to Mouth of Truth?

How do I find the Trevi Fountains?

Pardon me, I'm lost, how do I get to the Vatican City?

영화 '로마의 휴일'에 나오는 로마의 명소

영화 속 대사

Mr. Bradley : I'd like to go to Via Margutta 51 (Margutta 51 Street) near Piazza di Spagna?

Taxi Driver : Sure, Sir.

Mr. Bradley : Here is Via Margutta 51?

Taxi Driver : Yes, that's right.

2. 이탈리아(Italy) 소개

Italy is a land celebrated for the arts. And the arts that have attained their highest expression in Italy is the art of hospitality. The Italian welcome is as warm and traditional as a glass of fine wine. This comparison is proper, for travelers in ancient times gave the country its first name : Land of Wines. Italians are such good hosts because they get so much practice welcoming visitors from all over the world.

Italy is one of the most popular vacation countries in Europe, all seasons being good for a visit. In summer, Italy is an international playground, with visitors from all continents mingling with vacationing Italians at the famous

로마 전경

resorts. Spring comes early to Italy and autumn lingers - and so will the wise traveler who wants to enjoy at a more leisurely pace the art centers, the large cities and the holiday resorts such as those in the Lombardian lake region where spring and fall are ideal seasons.

Italy has always been our favorite country for tourism. It combines artistic treasures, friendly people, a beautiful language, fascinating history, and great food.

You could be a tourist here for your whole life and still there would have been something worthwhile up a little country road or behind an obscure church that you hadn't seen.

Sixty million Italians share a peninsula 800 miles long by about 100 miles wide (300% of Korea and 75% of the size of California). Rome is at about the same latitude as New York City, but the surrounding Mediterranean results in milder winters.

The main problem with Italian tourism is that while you are there trying to absorb medieval atmosphere and Roman history, 60 million Italians are trying to ignore it.

If you want to experience Italy as it once was, you have to either go to a town so small they don't have motorbikes (if you find one, let me know) or a place where cars are impractical such as in Venice and Capri.

1) The Mouth of Truth(진실의 입)

It is the "Bocca della Verità", which in English means the Mouth of Truth, an ancient stone mask from the Classical period that represents a river god with an open mouth, wide eyes and a flowing hair.

There was an old saying that if a liar puts their hand inside its mouth, they will lose it. This legend probably originates from Roman times. It is said that the rich wife of a Roman noble was accused of adultery. The woman denied the accusations, but her husband wanted to put her to the test by making her hand inside the stone mouth.

Knowing perfectly well that she was lying, the woman used a very clever strategy. In front of a group of curious bystanders who had gathered around the Mouth of Truth, the man who was actually her lover embraced her and kissed her. She pretended that she didn't know him and accused him of being a madman and the crowd chased him away.

When she put her hand into the mouth, the woman declared that she had never kissed any other man apart from her husband and the poor madman who had just kissed her. In this way she was certain that she hadn't lied and her hand was saved.

The betrayed husband saved her honour, but the Mouth of Truth lost its credibility and it is said that since that day it no longer carried out its function as a right judge.

The mask is so famous that even Hollywood honoured it in a film about the city called Roman Holiday. In one of the most memorable scenes, Gregory Peck, in front of a terrified Audrey Hepburn, daringly challenges the mask by putting his hand inside its mouth.

Even today, this ancient mask is the cause of queues of tourists who line up outside the beautiful Paleochristian church of Santa Maria in Cosmedin. The thrill of the risk is evidently too strong and you honestly can't resist putting your hand inside this harmless stone face and hope for the best.

2) Trevi Fountain(트레비 분수)

Trevi Fountain is a fountain in Rome, Italy. It is the largest Baroque fountain in the city and the most beautiful in the world. A traditional legend holds that if visitors throw a coin into the fountain, they are ensured a return to Rome.

The fountain is worldwide famous but many people do not know the history

and the secrets hidden behind its construction. It is time to do justice to this
extraordinary masterpiece of Italian art.

The design of the trevi fountain is based
on three architectural elements : a façade
made of travertine; statues of marble; a
see reef also made of travertine.

In the middle there is the statue of
Ocean, 5,8 meters high (16.4 feet high) carved by Pietro Bracci. The body is
muscular inclining to fatness. He has long and abundant beard. His look is
fiercely majestic and gentleman at the same time In his right hand he hold the
wand in act of command. His left hand holds a cloth around his pelvis to cover
his nudity.

He is carried on his tryumphal charriot by two horses. One horse is restless,
one is calm. Ocean is also standing in the median portion of a tryumphal arch.

In the left part of the arch there is the statue of Abundance holding the horn
of plenty. At her feet a toppled vase lies by a source of water. Above her there
is a relief showing Agrippa commanding his generals to build the acqueduct.

In the right portion there is the statue of Health, crowned by a wreth of laurel
and holding a cup a snake drinks from. Above her there is a relief showing a
Virgin lady indicating to soldiers the source of water.

There are also some animals : a snail lies on the marsh marygold and a lizard
is hiding in a ravine of the walls. On the right side of the sea cliff there is the
Coat of Arms of Monsignor Gian Galeazzo Caracciolo, President of the fountain
project for some years. It features a lion and the particular type of hat of Papal
Court prelates.

The fountain is backed by the Poli Palace that belonged to the Conti Family
dukes of Poli, a town in the Lazio Region. The palace was then inherited by the
Sforza Cesarini family and then to the Boncompagni family until 1885 when the
City Hall expropriated it. Today the palace houses the National Institute of
Graphic Art.

3) Vatican Palaces(바티칸 성당)

As early as the mid 9th century a small, fortified city surrounded the area around the ancient St Peter's Basilica, encircled by walls built by Leo IV (847-855), the so-called "Leonine city". Between the end of the 13th and the first decades of the 14th century, some establishments were built around the square courtyard, known as "Pappagallo". They were the first Vatican palaces.

After the Avignon Schism (1309-1377), no new buildings were erected until the end of the 15th century, when the palaces of Sixtus IV (1471-1484) were built. These include the Sistine Chapel, which takes its name from the Pope. Innocent VIII (1484-1492) also built some palaces, about 300 metres north of the Vatican basilica. Julius II (1503-1513) and his architect, Donato Bramante, had the idea of joining the two groups of buildings constructed by his predecessors, adding two magnificent, three-level courtyards.

During the 16th and 17th centuries, popes continued to work on and enlarge the Vatican palaces. Sixtus V (1585-1590) also built the palace where the present pope lives and where every Sunday at noon he stands at the window (the second from the right on the third floor), and blesses the crowd that gathers in the magnificent Vatican square.

3. 상황별 대화(Conversation by Situation)

At the Airport 1 : 체크인 데스크에서 좌석배정과 수화물 추가요금 청구 상황

비행기 티켓을 들고 있다고 해서 타고 갈 비행기의 좌석이 정해진 것은 아니다. 공항에 도착하는 즉시 체크인 데스크로 가서 좌석을 배정받는 것이 좋다. 사람에 따라 자주 일어서서 몸을 움직여야 할 경우 또는 화장실을 자주 가야 하는 경우가 있으므로 최대한 체크인 데스크에 일찍 가서 상황을 설명하고 원하는 좌석을 배정받는 것이 좋기 때문이다. 또한 가방은 기내에 가져갈 것과 화물로 보낼 것을 잘 구분해 두고 항공요금에 포함된 가방의 수나 무게에 대해서는 항공사마다 다르므로 반드시 사전에 확인해 두어 체크인 시 당황하는 일이 없도록 하자.

Check-In Worker	: Hello. Where are you flying today?
You	: Hi, I'm flying to London, England.
Check-In Worker	: Can I see your ticket and your passport, please?
You	: Sure. Here's my passport. And here's my e-ticket.
Check-In Worker	: Thank you. Would you like a window seat?
You	: No, I'd like an aisle seat please.
Check-In Worker	: OK, and is all this luggage yours?
You	: These two bags are mine.
Check-In Worker	: All right. One of your bags is overweight.... I'm going to have to charge you for the excess weight.
You	: I see. How much extra do I have to pay? And can I pay by credit card?
Check-In Worker	: €25 more, Sir, and yes, we do accept credit cards.

At the Airport 2 : 공항 내의 시설 및 이동 교통에 관해 문의하는 상황

You : Hi, where's the check-in counter for American Airlines?

Airport Worker : That's in terminal 2. This is terminal 1.

You : Is there a shuttle bus that goes between terminals?

Airport Worker : Yes, there's one right in front here.

You : Next to the taxi stand?

Airport Worker : Yes, that's right.

You : Thanks. How much time should I allow to check in?
(= How much time before my flight should I check in?)

Airport Worker : If you're on an international flight I believe you have to check-in 3 hours before your flight.

You : And for local flights?

Airport Worker : On those flights you have to check in 1 and a half hours before.

At the Airport 3 : 티켓 없이 체크인 데스크에 갔을 때의 상황

최근 들어 공항의 규모가 점점 커지고 복잡해지는 경향이 있다. 공항은 같은데 터미널이 여러 개 있을 수 있고 어떤 공항은 터미널 3과 터미널 4의 거리를 셔틀버스로 이동해야 할 정도로 크고 넓으므로 공항에 관한 정보도 미리 검색해 두는 것이 좋다.

Check-In Worker : Hi. Where are you flying today?

You : Hi, I'm flying to Miami, but I need a ticket.... Can I buy one here?

Check-In Worker : No, you'll have to go to the ticket counter.... That's over in terminal 3.

You : How do I get there?

Check-In Worker : You can walk there. The terminals are connected. Just turn right and go all the way to the end of this terminal and you'll be in Terminal 3.

(You Leave and Go to the Ticket Counter)

You : Hi there. I was told I could buy a ticket here?

Ticket Counter Worker : Yes you can. Where to?

You : I need a ticket to Miami, please, for today if possible.

Ticket Counter Worker : All right.... Yes, I can get you on the flight at 7:00 pm tonight, which arrives in Miami at 10:00 pm. This ticket is $650.

You : Do you have anything cheaper?

Ticket Counter Worker : No, not on such short notice, Sir. That's the lowest price I can get you for today or tomorrow.

At the Airport 4 : Customs/Immigration : 입국심사원의 질문대처 상황

출입국심사에서는 입국 목적, 머물 장소, 귀국일정 외 종종 직업에 대한 질문을 받는 경우도 있으므로 대비해 두도록 하자.

Border Guard : Welcome to Italy. Where do you live?

You : Germany.

Border Guard : And what's the purpose of your visit to Italy.

You : I'm going to visit my brother. He lives in Rome.

Border Guard : How long do you plan to stay in Rome?

You : About two weeks.

Border Guard : And what do you do back home?

You : Pardon me? I don't understand....

Border Guard : Your job... what do you do?

You : Oh, I'm a high-school teacher. I teach Physics and Chemistry.

Quiz

다음 대화에서 빈 칸에 들어갈 올바른 단어나 구는?

1. You : Hi, where's the check-in _____ for American Airlines?

① counter   ② control   ③ zone

Airport Worker : That's in terminal 2. This is terminal 1.

2. You : Is there a _____ that goes between terminals?

① transportation   ② shuttle bus   ③ vehicle

Airport Worker : Yes, there's one right in front here.

3. You : _____ to the taxi stand?

① Together   ② With   ③ Next

Airport Worker : Yes, that's right.

4. You : Thanks. How much time _____ to check in?
　　　(= How much time before my flight should I check in?)

① will I let   ② should I allow   ③ can I take

Airport Worker : If you're on an international flight I believe you have to
　　　　　　　　check-in 3 hours before your flight.

5. YOU : And for _____ flights?

　① local　　② country　　③ near

Airport Worker : On those flights you have to check in 1 and a half hours before.

 ## Vocabulary

1. declare = proclaim, announce, express, state, say
2. apt = proper
3. absorb = take in, soak, drink
4. obscure = unknown, little-known
5. ensure = guarantee, make sure
6. travertine = materials deposited from the spring, 온천의 침전물
7. establishments = buildings

Answers

1. counter　　　　2. shuttle bus　　　3. Next
4. should I allow　5. local

한국 레스토랑에서
(At the Restaurant in Korea)

- 영화 '경주'와 UNESCO 등재 '세계문화유산' 관광

1. 대화(Target Language)

레스토랑은 예약을 원칙으로 하나 그렇지 않을 경우에도 반드시 입구에서 웨이터의 안내를 기다린다. 의자에 착석할 때에는 웨이터가 의자를 뒤로 살짝 빼주는 경우가 있는데 그렇지 않을 경우 의자의 왼쪽으로 들어가 앉는다. 메뉴를 고를 경우 최대한 직원에게 물어보며 신중하게 주문하는 것이 좋다. 혹시 음식에 본인의 체질에 알레르기를 일으킬 수 있는 재료가 들어가 있는지를 확인하고 가격에 대한 이해를 확실히 하여 마지막 계산대에서 당황하는 일이 발생하지 않도록 유의하는 것이 좋다. 웨이터는 항상 고객의 즐거운 시간을 위해 주변에서 대기 중이므로 눈짓으로 부르거나 손을 살짝 올려서 의사표현하는 것이 좋다.

한정식 먹을 때 - At the Korean Restaurant

Waiter   : Welcome to Gyungju Bulgogi. Here are your menus. Today's specialty of the chef is grilled Galbi. I'll be back to take your order in a minute.

Waiter   : Are you ready to order?

Customer 1 : I'd like the grilled Galbi.

Waiter   : And you?

Customer 2 : I'll have a Bulgogi.

Waiter   : Would you like anything to drink?

Customer 1 : I'll have a rice water, please.

Waiter   : And for you?

Customer 2 : Just water, please.

호텔 내 레스토랑에서 - At the Restaurant

레스토랑에서 주문할 때에는 가능한 한 웨이터에게 오늘의 메뉴를 물어보고 조언을 구하는 것이 좋다. 레스토랑 주방에서는 계절에 맞는 혹은 특별히 좋은 재료를 준비하였을 경우 오늘의 요리로 선정하여 고객의 메뉴선택 시 추천하고 있다. 고객은 이럴 때 계절에 맞는 싱싱한 재료로 혹은 특별한 맛의 요리를 즐길 수 있어 좋다.

Waiter	:	Welcome to Antico's. Here are your menus. Today's special is grilled salmon. I'll be back to take your order in a minute.
Waiter	:	Are you ready to order?
Customer 1	:	I'd like the seafood spaghetti.
Waiter	:	And you?
Customer 2	:	I'll have a hamburger and fries.
Waiter	:	Would you like anything to drink?
Customer 1	:	I'll have a coke, please.
Waiter	:	And for you?
Customer 2	:	Just water, please.
Waiter	:	OK. So that's one seafood spaghetti, one hamburger and fries, one coke, and one water. I'll take your menus.
Waiter	:	Here is your food. Enjoy your meal.
Waiter	:	How was everything?
Customers 2	:	Delicious, thanks.
Waiter	:	Would you like anything for dessert?
Customer 1	:	No, just the bill please.

❀ 영화 '경주' 관광

영화 경주는 1박 2일 동안 박해일과 신민
아 두 주인공이 '경주'를 배경으로 해서 펼
치게 되는 엉뚱하고도 발랄한 여행담이다.
경주의 매력에 푹 빠진 중국의 장률 감독은
제작보고회에서 두 배우 마음속에 노인이 앉

아 있는 것 같다는 말을 했다고 한다. 그래서인지 경주의 고요한 배경과 전통찻집 분위기에 자연스럽게 잘 녹아들어 보는 내내 편안함을 느낄 수 있었다. 경주여행에서는 주인 없는 전통찻집을 비롯하여 여러 전통찻집이 있으니 경주 특유의 한정식과 더불어 전통찻집에서의 여유를 경험해 보는 것도 좋겠다.

UNESCO 등재 세계문화유산 관광

경주는 1995년 12월 석굴암, 불국사를 시작으로 2000년 11월 경주역사유적지구와 2010년 7월 한국의 역사마을인 양동마을이 UNESCO 세계문화유산에 등재됨으로써 외국인들의 방문이 눈에 띄게 증가하고 있다. 특히 경주역사지구에는 조각, 탑, 사지, 궁궐지, 왕릉, 산성을 비롯해 신라시대의 여러 뛰어난 불교유적과 생활유적이 집중적으로 분포되어 있다. 특히 7세기부터 10세기 사이의 유적이 많으며 이들 유적을 통해 신라 고유의 탁월한 예술성을 확인할 수 있다. 경주는 신라의 수도로 신라의 1000년 역사를 간직하고 있으며, 신라인의 생활문화와 예술감각을 잘 보여주는 곳이다. 경주역사지구는 총 5개 지구로 이루어져 있다. 다양한 불교유적을 포함하고 있는 남산지구, 옛 왕궁 터였던 월성지구, 많은 고분이 모여 있는 대릉원지구, 불교사찰 유적지인 황룡사지구, 방어용 산성이 위치한 산성지구가 이에 해당한다.

Asking for Directions

What do you know about Golden Crown on Silla?

What's the best way to get to the Bulkuksa and Sukgulam?

Can you give me directions to the traditional tea house behind Gyeongju National Museum?

영화 속 대화

Hyun : Isn't that odd looking at the tombs next to the house everyday?

Yoonhee : It is nearly impossible to live without seeing the tombs in Gyeongju.

2. 경주(Gyeongju) 소개

Gyeongju was the capital city of Silla from BC 57 to AD 935. The history of Gyeongju, once called Seorabeol or Seobul, is also the history of the thousand-year-old Silla kingdom. Gyeongju embraces Buddhism, science, and vibrant ancient culture that blossomed by the artistry of the Silla people, and the great spirits of Hwarangdo hat enabled the unification of the three kingdoms. Thus, Gyeongju is a UNESCO-designated city which should be preserved by the public. The evergreen spirit of Silla has been alive here for nearly a thousand years. With a thousand years of the evergreen spirit of Silla, Gyeongju is truly a museum without a roof.

1) Gyeongju Historic Areas(경주역사유적지구)

The Gyeongju Historic Areas contain a remarkable concentration of outstanding examples of Korean Buddhist art, in the form of sculptures, reliefs, pagodas, and the remains of temples and palaces from the flowering culture of Silla dynasty, in particular between the 7th and 10th century.

The Korean peninsula was ruled for almost 1,000 years (57 BCE-935 CE) by the Silla dynasty, and the sites and monuments in and around Gyeongju bear

제목 : 경주역사지구
설명 : 출처 : wikipedia, Marcopolis
경주역사지구

상세정보

- **국가** 대한민국(Korea, Republic of)
- **위치** 경상북도(慶尙北道)|||경주시(慶州市)
- **좌표** N35 47 20.004|||E129 13 36.012
- **등재연도** 2000년
- **등재기준**

기준 (ii) : 경주역사지구에는 불교건축 및 생활문화와 관련된 뛰어난 기념물과 유적지가 다수 분포해 있다.

기준 (iii) : 신라 왕실의 역사는 1000년에 이르며, 남산을 비롯해 수도 경주와 그 인근 지역에서 발견된 유물과 유적은 신라문화의 탁월함을 보여준다.

outstanding testimony to its cultural achievements. These monuments are of exceptional significance in the development of Buddhist and secular architecture in Korea.

The Mount Namsan Belt lies to the north of the city and covers 2,650 ha. The Buddhist monuments that have been excavated at the time of inscription include the ruins of 122 temples, 53 stone statues, 64 pagodas and 16 stone lanterns.

Excavations have also revealed the remains of the pre-Buddhist natural and animistic cults of the region. 36 individual monuments, including rock-cut reliefs or engravings, stone images and heads, pagodas, royal tombs and tomb groups, wells, a group of stone banner poles, the Namsan Mountain Fortress, the Poseokjeong Pavilion site and the Seochulji Pond, exist within this area.

The Wolseong Belt includes the ruined palace site of Wolseong, the Gyerim woodland which legend identifies as the birthplace of the founder of the Gyeongju Kim clan, Anapji Pond, on the site of the ruined Imhaejeon Palace, and the Cheomseongdae Observatory.

The Gyeongju Historic Area contain a remarkable concentration of outstanding examples of Korean Buddhist art, in the form of sculptures, reliefs, pagodas, and the remains of temples and places from the flowering, in particular between the 7th 10th centuries, of this form of unique artistic expression.

The Tumuli Park Belt consists of three groups of Royal Tombs. Most of the mounds are domed, but some take the form of a half-moon or a gourd. They contain double wood coffins covered with gravel, and excavations have revealed rich grave goods of gold, glass, and fine ceramics. One of the earlier tombs yielded a mural painting of a winged horse on birch bark.

Hwangnyongsa Belt consists of two Buddhist temples, Bunhwangsa Temple and the ruins of Hwangnyongsa Temple. Hwangnyongsa, built to the order of King Jinheung (540–576 CE) was the largest temple ever built in Korea, covering some 72,500m². An 80 m high, nine-storey pagoda was added in 645 CE. The pagoda in Bunhwangsa was built in 634 CE, using dressed block stones.

2) Seokguram Grotto and Bulguksa Temple(석굴암과 불국사)

Established in the 8th century on the slopes of Mount Toham, the Seokguram Grotto contains a monumental statue of the Buddha looking at the sea in the bhumisparsha mudra position.

With the surrounding portrayals of gods, Bodhisattvas and disciples, all realistically and delicately sculpted in high and low relief, it is considered a masterpiece of Buddhist art in the Far East.

The Temple of Bulguksa (built in 774) and the Seokguram Grotto form a religious architectural complex of exceptional significance.

Established in the 8th century under the Silla Dynasty, on the slopes of Mount Tohamsan, Seokguram Grotto and Bulguksa Temple form a religious architectural complex of exceptional significance.

Prime Minister Kim Dae-seong initiated and supervised the construction of the temple and the grotto, the former built in memory of his parents in his present life and the latter in memory of his parents from a previous life.

Seokguram is an artificial grotto constructed of granite that comprises an antechamber, a corridor and a main rotunda. It enshrines a monumental statue of the Sakyamuni Buddha looking out to sea with his left hand in dhyana mudra, the mudra of concentration, and his right hand in bhumisparsa mudra, the earth-touching mudra position.

Together with the portrayals of devas, bodhisattvas and disciples, sculpted in high and low relief on the surrounding walls, the statues are considered to be a masterpiece of East Asian Buddhist art. The domed ceiling of the rotunda and the entrance corridor employed an innovative construction technique that involved the use of more than 360 stone slabs.

Bulguksa is a Buddhist temple complex that comprises a series of wooden buildings on raised stone terraces. The grounds of Bulguksa are divided into three areas — Birojeon (the Vairocana Buddha Hall), Daeungjeon (the Hall of Great Enlightenment) and Geungnakjeon (the Hall of Supreme Bliss).

These areas and the stone terraces were designed to represent the land of Buddha. The stone terraces, bridges and the two pagodas — Seokgatap (Pagoda of Sakyamuni) and Dabotap (Pagoda of Bountiful Treasures) — facing the Daeungjeon attest to the fine masonry work of the Silla.

A wooden antechamber was also added and the interior of the grotto was sealed off by a wall of glass to protect it from visitors and changes in temperature.

The 1913-15 alterations to the grotto's original structure and subsequent modifications to address the problems caused by it require further study. Temperature and humidity control, and water ingress are carefully monitored and managed, and mitigation measures implemented as required.

Fire is the greatest threat to the integrity of the wooden buildings of the Bulguksa Tem-

다보탑(국보 20호)   석가탑(국보 21호)

ple, calling for systems for prevention and monitoring at the site.

Seokguram Grotto has been designated as National Treasure and- Bulguksa Temple has been designated as a Historic Site under the Cultural Heritage Protection Act. Any alterations to the existing form of the site require authorization.

They are included within the boundaries of Gyeongju National Park, in which there are restrictions on new construction. A Historic Cultural Environment Protection Area that extends 500 meters from the boundary of the site has also been established, in which all construction work must be pre-approved.

At the national level, the Cultural Heritage Administration (CHA) is responsible for establishing and enforcing policies for the protection of the property and buffer zone, allocating financial resources for conservation.

3) Wolseong Yangdong Village(양동마을)

Where the Confucian culture of the Joseon Dynasty is still alive Yangdong Village (Important Folk Material No. 189) This village, created by the Wolseong Son family clan and the Yeogang Lee family clan, consists of about 150 time-honored tiled-roof houses and thatched-roof houses.

Wolseong Yangdong Village is a typical noble village of the Joseon Dynasty. The

UNESCO World Heritage Site

entire village was designated as a cultural property. (It has one national treasure, four treasures, 12 important folk materials, two tangible cultural properties, one folk material, one cultural property material, and two folk cultural properties, and was selected as a UNESCO World Cultural Heritage on July 31, 2010.)

3. 상황별 대화(Conversation by Situation)

At the Restaurant 1 : Getting Seated - 입구에서 자리로 안내하기

Hostess : Hi and welcome to Roberto's. Do you have a reservation?

You   : No, we don't. Do you have any free tables this evening?

Hostess : Yes, we do... for 2?

You   : No, for 4 please. Some friends will be joining us.

Hostess : Right this way, please. (Shows You a Table)

You   : Could we get a table by the window?

Hostess : I'm sorry, but all those tables are reserved tonight...

You   : Could you please double check for us? Those tables are really nice.

Hostess : Certainly. I'll be back in a second... You're in luck! Someone just cancelled their reservation!

You   : That's great! Thank you very much for the research help.

At the Restaurant 2 : Ordering - 상세히 설명하며 주문받기

Waiter : Hi and welcome to Roberto's. Are you ready to order?

You   : Not yet, Give us a second, please.

Waiter : No problem. I'll be back in a couple of minutes....
        (After a Couple of Minutes) What would you like to order?

You   : How big are your portions?

Waiter : Very big, you'll definitely get full.

You : Perfect. And what does each order come with (= include)?

Waiter : Each order includes fries or a salad.

You : OK. I'll have the chicken breast, and for my wife... the trout.

Waiter : Great. And would you like fries or salad with that?

You : Fries for me and a salad for my wife.

Waiter : All right. I'll be right back with your order.

At the Restaurant 3 : Orderin - 음식을 기다리는 동안 음료 주문받기

Waiter : Would you like something to drink?

You : Yes, what kind of beer do you have?

Waiter : We have Budweiser, Miller, and Rolling Rock in bottles.

You : One Rolling Rock and one Budweiser, please... oh, and a glass of water.

Waiter : Alright. And... are you guys ready to order food, or should I give you couple of minutes?

You : We're ready. One order of the grilled calamari, and one order of the fried shrimp, please.

Waiter : And would you like fries with that?

You : Can we get a salad instead?

Waiter : Yes... or for $1 more you can get both....

You : Perfect, let's do that make it. Fries and salad with both.

Waiter : It shouldn't take too long.

At the Restaurant 4 : Ordering - 고객이 메뉴선택에 도움을 구할 때

Waiter : Are you ready to order?

You : Yes, we can't decide... what do you recommend?

Waiter : Well, our specialty is the Seafood Platter... it includes four different kinds of seafood....

You : Oh, no, I can't eat that.... I'm allergic to seafood! Anything else?

Waiter : Hmm.... Well, the Grilled Chicken is also quite good.

You : Perfect, we'll have two orders of that. It's not too spicy, is it?

Waiter : No, it's pretty mild. And what would you like to drink?

You : What kind of juice do you have?

Waiter : Orange, mango, and pineapple.

You : Two pineapple juices please. Oh... and an ashtray.

Waiter : I'm sorry, but smoking is not allowed in the restaurant.

At the Restaurant 5 : Eating a Meal - 메인식사 후 디저트 주문받기

Waiter : Is everything alright?

You : Yes, that was a really great food. We both loved it.

Waiter : I'm glad you liked it. Is there anything else I can get you?

You : Yes, two coffees... and do you have a dessert menu?

Waiter : Certainly. I'll be right back with that.

You : Oh, and be sure to give our compliments to the chef.... The meal was fantastic.

Waiter : I'll be sure to do that. (The Waiter Comes Back with the Menus) Here you go.

You : Thanks. Is the cheesecake good?

Waiter : Yes, it's very tasty. Our customers usually love it.

You : OK. Bring us two pieces, please.

At the Restaurant 6 : Eating/Bad Service - 고객의 컴플레인 발생 상황

Waiter : Is everything alright?

You   : Well, no, actually the soup is a little cold.... Could you ask them to heat it up for me?

Waiter : Sure. I'll be right back with that.

You   : Oh, and I asked for a salad, not fries.

Waiter : I'm sorry about that, I'll get your salad as well.

You   : One last thing, I asked for a Coke about 15 minutes ago.

Waiter : Yes, I totally forgot about that. It's a very busy time now.

(10 Minutes Later)

You   : Excuse me, I'm still waiting for my Coke.

Waiter : Oh, right! I'll get that for you right away....

You   : Never mind(= forget about it), we're leaving.

At the Restaurant 7 : Finishing a Meal/Paying - 식사 후 계산 관련 대화

Waiter : Can I get you anything else?

You   : Just the check/bill, please.

Waiter : Sure. I'll be right back with that.... Did you want to pay separately?

You   : No, you can put it all on one check/bill.

Waiter : (Brings the Check) There you go. Thanks.

You   : Excuse me, do we pay here or at the cash register?

Waiter : You can pay me.

You   : OK, and the tip isn't included in the check, correct?

Waiter : No, Sir, it isn't.

You   : (You Give the Money to the Waiter) There you go. Thanks. You've been very helpful.

Quiz

다음 대화에서 빈 칸에 들어갈 올바른 단어나 구는?

Hostess : Hi and welcome to Roberto's. Do you have a reservation?

1. You : No, we don't. Do you have _____ this evening?

   ① tables waiting   ② somewhere to sit down   ③ any free tables

   Hostess : Yes, we do... for 2?

2. You : No, for 4 please. Some friends will be _____ us.

   ① eating   ② joining   ③ sitting

   Hostess : Right this way, please. (Shows You a Table)

3. You : Could we get a table _____?

   ① by the window   ② window   ③ with window

   Waiter : Hi and welcome to Roberto's. Are you ready to order?

4. You : Not yet, _____, please.

   ① give us a second   ② more time   ③ more time is needed

   Waiter : No problem. I'll be back in a couple of minutes....
              (After a Couple of Minutes) What would you like to order?

5. You : How big are your _____?

① foods   ② portions   ③ plates

Waiter : Very big, you'll definitely get full.

6. You : Perfect. And what does each order _____ (=include)?

① come to   ② come by   ③ come with

Waiter : Each order includes fries or a salad.

Waiter : Are you ready to order?

7. You : Yes, we can't decide... what do you _____?

① say   ② decide   ③ recommend

Waiter : Well, our specialty is the Seafood Platter... it includes four different kinds of seafood....

8. You : Oh, no, I can't eat that.... I'm _____ to seafood! Anything else?

① allergic   ② allergy   ③ an allergy

Waiter : Hmm.... Well, the Grilled Chicken is also quite good.

9. You : Perfect, we'll have two orders of that. It's not too _____, is it?

① mild   ② cold   ③ spicy

Waiter : No, it's pretty mild. And what would you like to drink?

Vocabulary

1. specialty = specialty dish, Today's specialty of the chef
2. rice water = water from boiled rice
3. bill = invoice, check

Answers

1. any free tables	2. joining	3. by the window
4. give us a second	5. portions	6. come with
7. recommend	8. allergic	9. spicy

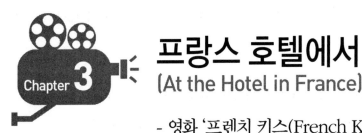

프랑스 호텔에서
(At the Hotel in France)

- 영화 '프렌치 키스(French Kiss)' 관광

1. 호텔에서의 대화(Target Language at the Hotel)

관광 중 숙박장소는 고된 하루의 시작과 마무리를 위한 에너지 재충전의 장소이며 호텔의 경우 게스트가 단 1박을 하더라도 이를 위해 바늘과 실을 담은 소잉 키트(sewing kit)에서부터 잠옷까지 100여 가지의 소품을 준비하고 있는 곳이다. 그러므로 호텔에서 사용되는 프런트 클럭, 하우스 맨 혹은 룸서비스 직원, 국제전화 연결 및 전화 후 메시지 확인을 위해 필요한 경우에 대비하여 가능한 한 많은 표현을 익혀두자.

다음은 고객이 객실에서 프런트로 전화하여 지난밤 불편사항을 전달하며 객실 내에 비치되어 있는 미니바에 있는 물품의 가격에 관해 물어본다. 최근 미니바에 들어 있는

물품의 가격이 시중보다 훨씬 비싸므로 사용하는 고객이 줄어들자 미니바 내부를 비워두는 호텔이 증가하고 있다.

You	: I can't open the window in my room. It seems to be stuck.
Hotel Clerk	: I'll get someone to take a look at it. Anything else?
You	: Yes, how much is the beer in the mini bar? I couldn't find a price list.
Hotel Clerk	: It's $5 a bottle. Anything else?
You	: Yes, could you tell the people in the room next to us to be quiet at night? They were screaming all night and we couldn't sleep.
Hotel Clerk	: Absolutely. I'll ask them to keep the noise down. Anything else?
You	: No, I think that's it... What time do we have to check out tomorrow?
Hotel Clerk	: You'll have to leave your room by 12:00 pm.
You	: OK. And is there somewhere we can hang out until the evening?
Hotel Clerk	: Yes, you can leave them in our storage room.

🎞 영화 French Kiss

순진한 역사 선생 케이트(맥 라이언)는 의사인 찰리(티모시 허튼)와 약혼한 사이로 그와 새 가정을 꾸밀 꿈에 부풀어 있다. 고소공포증으로 비행기 타기를 무서워하는 케이트는 세미나 참석차 파리에 가자는 찰리의 제의를 거절하고 집에 홀로 남는다.

얼마 후, 케이트는 찰리로부터 사랑하는 여자가 생겼다는 전화를 받는다. 그 길로 비행기를 타고 파리로 가던 중 건달같이 보이는 뤼크(케빈 클라인)라는 남자가 케이트에

게 관심을 보인다. 뤼크는 어린애같이 순진무구한 케
이트에게 자꾸 끌리는 자신을 발견한다. 뤼크의 전략
대로 찰리와 만난 케이트는 찰리가 새로 사귄 여자를
버리고 다시 자신에게 돌아오겠다고 하자 그에게 환
멸을 느낀다.

그리고는 포도밭을 경영해서 건전한 삶을 찾겠다는
뤼크의 원을 이루어주기 위해 이제까지 저금해 온
45,000여 달러를 톡톡 털어서 뤼크가 훔친 다이아몬
드 목걸이 값을 지불해 주고 떠난다. 이 사실을 알게
된 뤼크는 케이트를 뒤쫓아가 사랑을 고백하고, 케이
트 또한 이번 경험을 통하여 진실한 사랑이 뭔지 깨닫
고 뤼크를 받아들인다.

Asking for Directions

Could you tell me how to get to Montmartre?

Excuse me! How do I get to the Eiffel Tower?

Pardon me, I'm lost, where is the nearest subway station from here?

영화 속 대사

Welcome to Air Canada,

nonstop service Toronto to Paris.

Our flying time today is an estimated seven hours, twenty minutes.

Check that your seat belt is fastened and your chair back is in the upright position.

We will be taking off shortly.

Kate...

Yes?

Are you prepared to have a pleasant flight?

Yes.

Tell me, Kate.

What are you thinking about?

2. 파리(Paris) 소개

Paris is one of the birthplaces of photography and a city whose casual beauty makes for rich material to anyone willing to walk around slowly and observe carefully. It could be that your eyes will settle on a bit of sculpture on a building facade. Or the arrangement of goods in a shop.

1) Standard Paris Photos

If you want to convince your friends that you really were in the City of Light, make sure that you've got some photos of Notre Dame, the area around Ile de la Cite, the Tour Eiffel, and the Champs Elysees with the Arc de Triomphe in the background. There is a variety of ways to make these more interesting than the standard point-and-shoot image. Start by using black and white film. All the great photographers of Paris (e.g., Atget, Cartier-Bresson, Doisneau, Kertesz) worked in black and white.

Try using wide-angle lenses with people in the foreground and monuments in back. Parisians are reliably stylish and tourists are reliably clownish. Either way, you've got something entertaining and unique in the foreground. If you're willing to lug a tripod, use a long telephoto lens to compress multiple buildings into flat patterns. If you're emulating Cartier-Bresson and traveling light with just a 50mm lens, it is even more vital that you get comfortable smiling at passersby and snapping their pictures.

2) People Looking at Art

Paris is the ultimate place to get photos of people viewing and reacting to art. There is sculpture throughout the city and the museums tend to be camera-friendly if not flash-friendly. The easiest museum in which to create dramatic images of art, people, and structure is the Musee d'Orsay, a converted train station housing art from 1850 through World War I. Another good choice is Centre Pompidou, the modern art museum and cultural center.

3) Photographic Exhibitions

Pick up a copy of Reponses Photo at a newsstand and turn to the Actuexpos (L'Actualite des Expositions) section for a list of museum and gallery photo exhibitions throughout France, organized by region.

4) Disneyland Paris

A 40-minute RER ride from the center of Paris and you're in people photography heaven : Disneyland. Try black and white to focus attention on the bizarre attitudes of the crowd, the pained expressions of those who've waited on line for hours. I keep meaning to take a Fuji 617 panoramic camera in there.

5) Cemeteries

For the graves of great artists, marked by fine stone carving, Parisian cemeteries are unexcelled. Visit Cimetiere de Montmartre, the resting place of Hector Berlioz, Henrich Heine, Vaslav Nijinsky, Jacques Offenbach, and Francois Truffaut.

Then move south to the Cimetiere du Montparnasse, where you find the graves of Frederic Auguste Bartholdi (Statue of Liberty), Charles Baudelaire, Samuel Beckett, Andre Citroen, Alfred Dreyfus (Dreyfus Case), Man Ray, Guy de Maupassant, Camille Saint-Saens, Jean-Paul Sartre and Simone de Beauvoir.

You can end your day east of downtown at the Cimitiere du Pere Lachaise (16 Rue du Repos; Metro : Pere Lachaise). Honore de Balzac, Sarah Bernhardt,

Frederic Chopin, Moliere, Yves Montand, Jim Morrison, Edith Piaf, Marcel Proust, and Oscar Wilde await you.

6) Montmartre/Sacre Coeur

Except in winter, the hill of Montmartre is worthwhile for photographing tourists interacting with artists working on the street.

7) Suggested Day around the Eiffel Tower

Get to the Tour Eiffel when it opens (9:00 am in July and August; 9:30 am the rest of the year). Take some photos from the top and around the base while the sunlight is still coming from an interesting angle.

Proceed to Rue Cler, a pedestrian street market for photographs of people shopping, food and flowers for sale. Save your appetite, though, for the cafe at the Musee Rodin.

Proceed on foot to the Musee Rodin at 77 Rue de Varenne. Take some pictures of the Rodin sculptures in the garden. The little cafe in the garden serves nice light lunches in a tranquil environment. As a bonus for Americans, the interior part of the cafe is completely non-smoking.

If you still have energy left, double back to the Hotel des Invalides. This complex, built on an inhuman scale, is not a great place for photography but it contains the important Dome Church within which lies Napoleon's Tomb as well as an interesting army museum. The most unusual part of the museum is a collection of relief maps (Musee des Plans-Reliefs). The light levels are too low for photography but it is interesting nonetheless.

If you're in the mood for more art, there is a lovely small museum devoted primarily to the works of Aristide Maillol at 59 Rue de Grenelle on your way toward the Sevres-Babylone Metro stop.

You can end your day in the brasserie at the historic Hotel Lutetia, right on top of the Sevres-Babylone Metro stop and across the square from the Bon Marche department store.

8) Skip the Marais

If you're short on time, you can skip the Marais, every guidebook's favorite Paris neighborhood. This is a gentrified-in-the-1960s quarter of narrow streets that lacks the authenticity of the rest of down-town Paris. For example, there is a street containing some kosher food shops, Rue  des Rosiers. You're supposed to see Hassidim walking down the streets in dreadlocks, stocking up for Shabbat. In reality, any Jews that you see are most likely to be from New York and clad in jeans and a T-shirt.

The Marais contains some important museums. The Musee Picasso displays the painter's personal collection of works, i.e., stuff that didn't sell. The museum is further notable for being perhaps the only museum in Paris that has bothered to put up an English translation of its signage. The Museee Carnavalet is even more interesting, though photography seems to be forbidden. This contains paintings and rooms from various periods in Parisian history.

9) English Bookstore

Brentano's at 37 Avenue L'Opera is better and bigger than the average mall bookstore in the US. WH Smith at 248 Rue de Rivoli is also a good choice for selection. If you want a conversation and a bit of history to go with your Danielle Steele novel, visit Shakespeare and Company, 37 Rue de la Bucherie.

10) Other Shops

In terms of the way that goods are organized and displayed, Paris is one of the world's finest shopping cities. And the Parisians are thoughtful curious shoppers. This leads to some good photo opportunities. The area around Madeleine contains Fauchon, the most

famous name in Paris gourmet foods, and also a variety of more specialized competitors.

A particularly interesting kind of shopping experience is the 19th century gallery or "passage". There are a bunch of these just to the east of the Opera Garnier.

Another interesting theme is the exotic and unfamiliar brand names that you'll find in Paris.

11) Hotels

If you need Internet connectivity from your room, there are but few choices. Sofitel Arc de Triomphe will supposedly have 10base-T jacks in every room for Ethernet- based connectivity by the end of February 2001.

If you don't need Internet connectivity or perhaps you're willing to struggle with a modem and a European ISP, your choices are varied. It is best to decide on a neighborhood first.

If you're interested in nightlife and shopping, the Opera Quarter is fabulous. I've stayed in the Millenium Hotel, 12 Boulevard Haussman, www. stay-with-us.com,

opera@mill-cop.com, (01) 49 49 16 00. It is conveniently situated for the gourmet, with a McDonald's to the left, another McDonald's across the street, and a third down the Boulevard des Italiens.

Nearly 20 cinema screens are within

a 5-minute walk (look for "VO" or "version originale" if you don't want to strain to understand a French-dubbed "VF" or "version francaise" of your Hollywood classic) and a bunch of good all-night or late-night brasseries. I've never stayed in the Ambassador Hotel, next door at 16 Boulevard Haussman, but it is reputed to be excellent as well. From either hotel, it is about a 20-minute (interesting) walk to the Louvre and Notre Dame.

If you want to wake up and stroll by the river, walk into an art museum, or visit Notre Dame, you can't do better than a hotel smack in the middle of the Ile St-Louis. These will all be small; don't expect the facilities of a palace or business hotel. The DK guide recommends Hotel des Deux-Iles, (01) 43 26 13 35, and Hotel du Jeu de Paume, (01) 43 26 14 18.

12) Restaurants

The Michelin Red Guides are the most reliable source for restaurants throughout Europe. A Michelin Red Guide Paris is a bit cumbersome to carry around a city, however, and tends not to bother rating quick and simple places. One useful strategy for Paris is to stop into a good hotel and ask the concierge for a recommendation in the neighborhood.

13) Opera

Le Petit Bofinger, 20 Boulevard Mont-martre, is friendly, open fairly late, and has a large non-smoking section at the back of the restaurant. Menus at $15 and $25.

Just beyond the north wall of the Palais Royal, Le Grand Colbert is a beautifully decorated brasserie (2 Rue Vivienne; (01) 42 86 87 88).

14) Bottom Line

There are seven Michelin 3-star restaurants in Paris and several thousand crummy crepe or couscous joints. Those are your starting odds. Unlike the small towns of France, highish prices won't guarantee quality food and service. A crowded brasserie on the Champs Elysees may merely be serving tourists too lazy to ask around, check the guidebooks, or walk a bit. Even the locals aren't necessarily discriminating; fast food chains proliferate and prosper throughout the city.

The Dorling Kindersley guide is also good about indicating whether or not photography is allowed within a site. Finally, the guide contains a Metro/RER map on the back cover, a small street atlas, restaurant recommendations, and hotel listings. Somehow the end result is just a bit weak for planning purposes but it is perfect to keep in your pocket.

15) Getting Around

Though the Metro is efficient, taxis in Paris are surprisingly cheap, practical, and scenic. Within the tourist areas, a one-way taxi trip is unlikely to cost more than $10. For long trips by yourself, though, you can save the big bucks by taking the RER, a kind of commuter rail.

3. 상황별 대화(Conversation by Situation)

At the Hotel 1 : Checking in - 객실 뷰에 따라 객실요금이 차이나는 상황

You   : Hello, My name is Dennis. I have a reservation.

Hotel Clerk : Certainly, Sir. (Checks the Reservation System) Yes, would you like a room facing the pool or the ocean?

You   : Is there a difference in price between the two?

Hotel Clerk : Yes, the rooms that face the ocean are $100 per night, while the ones facing the pool are $80 per night.

You	: OK, I'll go with the one facing the ocean, please.
Hotel Clerk	: And you would like that for three nights, correct?
You	: Yes, that's right.
Hotel Clerk	: I'll have the porter bring up your bags.
You	: No, that's fine, I'll do it myself.

At the Hotel 2 : Checking in - 객실을 미리 둘러보고 체크인을 원하는 상황

Hotel Clerk	: We have you booked in room #303.
You	: Would it be possible to see the room?
Hotel Clerk	: Of course, it's upstairs to your right. Here's the key.

(You Look at the First Room)

Hotel Clerk	: So, do you like the room?
You	: Well, it's a little dark. Do you have any that are brighter?
Hotel Clerk	: Yes, we do have one, but it faces the street, so it's a little noisy.
You	: Could I take a look at that one?
Hotel Clerk	: Of course. It's room # 305 and it's upstairs to your left. Here's the key.

(You Look at the Other Room)

You	: That room is perfect. I'll take it.
Hotel Clerk	: That'll be $120.
You	: I have to pay advance?
Hotel Clerk	: Yes, that's our policy.

Expressions Used to Ask for Repeats - 다시 한번 말해 달라는 표현

Excuse me.

Pardon me.

Please say that again.

Can you repeat that please?

I'm sorry.

I'm sorry, I didn't catch that.

Dialogues about Asking for Repeats - 반복 질문하는 상황

Guest : Could I have more soap in the bathroom?

Staff : I'm sorry. Could you repeat that, please?

Guest : I need more soap.
　　　　 Which way to the gym?

Staff : Pardon me.

Guest : How do I get to the gym?

Guest : I'd like to schedule a tennis game.

Staff : I'm sorry Sir. Could you say that again.

Guest : I want to reserve a tennis court.

Quiz

다음 대화에서 빈 칸에 들어갈 올바른 단어나 구는?

1. You : Hello, my name is Dennis. I have a _____.

① check-in   ② reservation   ③ reserve

Hotel Clerk : Certainly, Sir. (Checks the Reservation System) Yes, would you like a room facing the pool or the ocean?

2. You : Is there _____ between the two?

① a difference in price   ② more expensive   ③ cheaper

Hotel Clerk : Yes, the rooms that face the ocean are $100 per night, while the ones facing the pool are $80 per night.

3. You : OK, _____ with the one facing the ocean, please.

① make me   ② I'll go   ③ do it

4. You : Can you _____ a good restaurant around here?

① recommend   ② say   ③ tell

Hotel Clerk : Hmm... there aren't any restaurants around here....

5. You : What about _____?

① in city   ② in the city   ③ central

Hotel Clerk : There are a lot of good restaurants in the area of the city called Uptown. If you go to Central Avenue, you'll see about 10 different restaurants, all of which are highly recommendable.

6. You : Great! How do we _____ Central Avenue from here?

① come at   ② arrive in   ③ get to

 **Vocabulary**

1. stick = attach, affix, paste, glue, be stuck
2. check out = pay the check or bill and go out, investigate, look into,
3. check in = go through the entry procedure (in a hotel or plane), book into a check-in front in a hotel, a check-in counter in an airport
4. hang out = idle away, kill time, spend time
5. face = confront
6. book in = check in

We have you booked in room #303.라는 문장에서 have는 '가지다'라는 의미의 소유동사가 아니라 사역동사로 목적어 you가 호텔에 들어가는 과정을 처리해 주었다는 의미

Answers

1. reservation	2. a difference in price	3. I'll go
4. recommend	5. in city	6. get to

라스베이거스에서 길 물어보기
(Asking Directions in Las Vegas)

Chapter 4

- 영화 '레인맨(Rain Man)' 관광

1. 대화(Target Language)

영어를 배우는 동안 가장 이해하기 어려운 표현 중 하나가 길을 묻고 답하는 것이라고 한다. 이것은 아마 생활환경 탓이 아닐까 싶다. 유럽의 도로와 길은 대부분 블록으로 나눠져 있어 약도 하나로 길을 찾는 것이 쉬운 반면 우리나라는 최근에야 생활 편리를 위해 주소 정비가 이루어지고 있기 때문이다. 다행히 길에 대한 문의와 답하는 표현은 반복 연습해 두면 두고두고 기억에 남을 테니 집중해 보자.

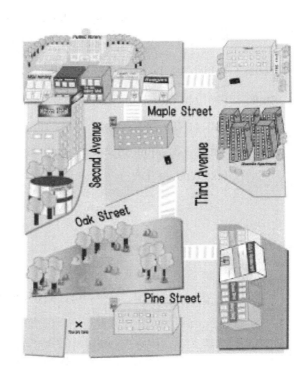

Guest : Could you tell me how to get to the Spa?

Staff : Take this passage-way and go down the steps on your right. At the bottom of the steps there is a wooden bridge. Go over the bridge and turn right. Follow the path until you get to the Spa. It's about 40 miles from the bridge.

Guest : How do I find the Thai restaurant?

Staff : Just follow the pathway to the left of the reception desk in the lobby. The walk-way will take you directly to the Thai Restaurant.

Guest : Which way do I go to get to the Beach Hotel?

Staff : From the Bell Desk in the Lobby, turn left and follow the path on the right and go past the pond and up the steps. From there, walk straight across the beach road, the Beach Hotel will be right in front of you.

Guest : Pardon me, I'm lost, how do I get to the gym?

Staff : From the main lobby, walk away from the beach and take the first staircase on your right down. The staircase is next to the portrait center. The gym is on your right at the bottom of the stairs.

Guest : Which is the best route to the LA?

Staff : Get on the road over there and drive north on the Beltway. At the end of the beach road, turn right on the Beltway and drive east. Take the IS 3 about 4 miles and turn right on the 4020. That road will take you to LA.

🎞 영화 '레인맨(Rain Man)' 관광

찰리(톰 크루즈)는 갑작스런 아버지의 죽음으로 자폐증 환자인 형 레이먼(더스틴 호프먼)을 돌봐야만 유산의 절반을 가질 수 있게 된다. 300만 달러의 유산을 독점하기 위해 레이먼과 만난 찰리는 그와 라스베이거스로 떠난다. 그러나 비행기를 탈 수 없는 레이먼 때문에 3시간이면 갈 거리를 3일이나 걸려 자동차로 대륙을 횡단한다.

　라스베이거스에서 도박을 하던 중 찰리는 레이먼의 비상한 기억력을 알게 되고 그의 능력을 이용해 돈을 벌어 그의 사업 부채를 청산할 수 있게 되고 예전부터 운전이 하고 싶었던 레이먼에게 고물차를 운전하게 해 준다. 찰리는 2주일간의 레이먼과의 여행을 통해 진정한 형제애를 깨닫고 레이먼을 자신이 돌보려 하지만 자폐 증상이 심한 레이먼은 다시 요양소로 돌아가게 되는데…

Asking for Directions

Could you tell me how to get to Binion's Horseshoe in downtown?

How do I find the Fremont Stree?

(Then,) turn left/right at the traffic light.

영화 속 대화

Charlie : That's a bed. That's your bed. I had'em put it up there especially... for you. Right by the window, just the way you like it.

Raymond : Bed by the window.

Charlie : That's right. Go on up.

Raymond : Yeah.

Charlie : Just the way you like it, isn't it?

Raymond : Yeah.

Charlie : Look at you with all those lights, Ray. Mr. Vegas!

You are Mr. Vegas now, man! What do you think, huh?

Raymond : There's a lot of lights out there. It's.. very sparkly. Very twinkly.

2. 라스베이거스(Las Vegas) 소개 : 마이스(MICE) 산업의 중심지

Las Vegas is

- the fastest-growing city in the United States (1999)
- the most popular tourist destination for Hawaiians
- close to awe-inspiring canyons that are ripe for photographers

Beyond the tourist areas of Downtown and The Strip, Las Vegas sprawls out into the desert. It is a horrifying vision of an American future where children will grow up knowing only strip malls, franchises, walled-and-planned communities, and 110-degree summer heat.

As a tourist destination, Las Vegas is a paradise. Hotels are reasonably cheap, Broadway shows play nightly in theaters with cupholders and ample free parking, and the general level of public spectacle is higher than anywhere else in the United States.

If you want to see nature by day and Cirque de Soleil by night, Las Vegas is 45-minutes from Red Rock Canyon, two hours from Zion National Park, and 2.5 hours from Cathedral Gorge State Park.

라스베이거스

1) Downtown Vegas

Downtown Vegas, which few tourists visit, contains the oldest, tackiest, and in many ways most interesting sights of the city. On the Strip, you drive from one enormous parking structure and theme-park sized casino to another. On Fremont Street, you walk from casino to casino, enticed by barkers. To boost tourism, the city has built an enormous canopy over four blocks of the slightly seedy area and dubbed it "The Fremont Street experience". At night there may be light shows with music projected against this canopy.

2) Gambling

MIT folks tend not to do anything unless they are really good at it. Being good at gambling means being able to achieve a positive expectation at blackjack. If you don't count cards but are a good player, your expectation is -2%. That means if you bet $1.00, you expect to have $0.98 at the end of a round.

This would be the best that you could do if the casino were dealing from an infinite deck. However, the casinos typically use between two and six decks of cards, all shuffled together.

If there are six decks and you've seen 24 cards with a value of 8 dealt out, you know that there won't be any more coming. By using this information, a good player can improve the odds to +2%, so that a $1.00 bet yields an average of $1.02.

It is illegal to bring a computer into the casino and therefore you have to learn to compute all of these probabilities in your head. This is a laborious process that takes members of the MIT Blackjack Team months. Once you've learned the method you can beat the casino consistently.

However, if the casino thinks that you're counting, they can throw you out. Sound unfair? The casinos can actually throw you out for any reason at any time. They own enough politicians that the laws are friendly to them in this way. The really bad thing is to be "read" where some goons grab you and read you a document that says if you return you'll be trespassing.

Then the casinos can put you in jail. So card counters become adept at disguise via wigs, contact lenses, etc. They also learn to disguise their play so it isn't obvious that they are counting (this reduces their odds).

Another winnable game is poker. You play against other people in a room provided by the casino. The casino takes a percentage of the play but basically if you're the best player in the room you will win a lot of money.

Roulette is winnable if you use a computer. The casino allows bets to be placed after the ball and wheel are spinning and almost until the point at which the ball drops into a slot. It isn't possible to perfectly predict the final slot from the ball and wheel's current position and velocity, but you don't need to be right. Roulette pays off 36 : 1 so if the computer is right even a small portion of the time, the expectation can be +25% or even higher.

Personally I never wanted to learn how to win so I don't gamble. If I were to gamble, I would do it at Binion's Horseshoe in downtown Las Vegas. Binion's has all the grit of old Las Vegas, before so many Disneyland-esque hotels were built on the Strip. The founder, Benny Binion, is a legendary figure. His son Ted was murdered on September 17, 1998 by his girlfriend and her lover. The girlfriend, Sandy Murphy, was an former topless dancer half Binion's age. The death was arranged to look accidental, with Binion taking an overdose of Xanax, a prescription tranquilizer. Binion's sister prompted an investigation : "That was not Ted.... Ted would be the first one to tell you that his drug of choice was heroin." (full story : http://www.lasvegassun.com/dossier/crime/binion/).

It is very difficult to get a camera into a casino's gambling area. The casinos are worried that folks who've told their wives that they've gone to Schenectady will be afraid that they'll show up in the background on someone's snapshot and the wife will learn what they've done with Junior's college fund.

3) What to See at Night

Cirque de Soleil has two shows in Las Vegas. "Mystere", at Treasure Island, is the older show and easier to get tickets for. "O" is newer and plays at the Bellagio. Get tickets as far in advance as possible. Mystere box office : (702) 894-7710; O box office : (888) 488-7111.

If the shows are sold out, you can pay $100+ extra and buy tickets from a broker, such as www.viptickets.com (1-800-328-4253).

If you're on a budget, you can entertain yourself adequately at no cost by visiting

- Downtown Las Vegas (Fremont Street) to see the packed-together neon lights and massive canopy
- Strip-side shows such as the artificial volcano at the Mirage, the musical fountains at Bellagio, the pirate battle in front of Treasure Island, etc.

4) Where to Stay

The Desert Inn ("DI") is right on the Strip and has a reputation as the place for sophisticated Las Vegas travelers. The casino is very small, the pool is large, the spa and exercise machines are the best, the 18-hole golf course in back is unique. Room rates are a touch higher than in other hotels but the rooms are big and have sliding glass doors that open. More info : www.thedesertinn.com

If you want to be crass and nouveau riche, the current favored casino-hotel is Bellagio : www.bellagiolasvegas.com

5) Where to Eat

The Desert Inn and Bellagio have the best fancy restaurants. Luxor has a great Chinese restaurant.

6) When to Visit

June, July, and August are bad, with an average high temperature of over 100 degrees. April, May, and October are just about prefect, with average high temperatures between 70 and 80. It can be chilly in the middle of winter, though skiing is possible on nearby Mount Charleston.

Be mindful of trade shows that can fill up the entire city. Two big ones are COMDEX (irrelevant side note : my friend Richard and I built www.comdex.com, a dynamic database-backed Web site with online schedule planning and show reservations, back in 1996) and the Consumer Electronics Show (CES). Below are some snapshots from my last trip to CES when my company's booth happened to be next to the pre-recorded adult video area.

3. 상황별 대화(Conversation by Situation)

Asking for Directions : Conversations 1 - 은행을 찾아가는 상황

You : Pardon me, is there a bank around here?

Person on Street : Yeah, there's one on this street, just keep walking straight for two blocks and you'll see it.

You : Which side of the street is it on?

Person on Street : It's on this side.... Are you looking for a particular bank?

You : No, any bank will do. I just need to exchange some money.

Person on Street : Oh.... You know there's also a currency exchange place not too far from here....

You : Oh there is? How do I get there?

Person on Street : It's just one block past the bank that I told you about. When you come to the bank, just keep going straight.

You : Perfect. Thanks for your help!

Asking for Directions : Conversations 2 - 레스토랑 가는 길을 문의하는 상황

You : Pardon me, do you know where Emilio's Restaurant is?

Person on Street : Emilio's.... Isn't that on Beverly?

You	:	I'm not sure. Someone told me it was around here.
Person on Street	:	Yeah, I know the place.... It is on Beverly. OK, you have to turn around and drive that way... and when you get to Beverly Blvd, turn right.
You	:	So, I have to make a U-turnaround and go back the other way?
Person on Street	:	Yes, until you get to Beverly Blvd.
You	:	And how many blocks is that from here?
Person on Street	:	I'm not sure, but it's about 1 mile, more or less.
You	:	And then I make a left. on Beverly?
Person on Street	:	No, then you turn right on Beverly.... And you'll see the restaurant on your left.

Asking for Directions : General Terms/Phrases - 길을 묻는 다양한 표현

1) Q : Do I keep going straight?
   A : No, you have to turn at the next intersection.

2) Q : Do I turn right at the next set of lights?
   A : No, turn left.

3) Q : Is it too far to walk there?
   A : Yes, you'll have to take a bus.

4) Q : Can you show me where it is on the map?
   A : Sure, it's right here.

5) Q : Is the post office next to the bank?
   A : No, it's across the bank.

6) Q : Do I take the next exit?
   A : No, take the one after that.

7) Q : Am I going the right way?
   A : Yes, you are.

8) Q : Am I going in the right direction?

   A : No, you have to turn around.

9) Q : Is this the way/road to Indianapolis?

   A : No, you're on the wrong highway.

10) Q : Where's the nearest gas station/bank/hotel, etc.?

   A : It's about 2 blocks from here.

Direction in Strange and New Places

여행 중이 아니더라도 길을 묻거나 길을 알려주는 일은 일상에서도 종종 일어난다. 잘 아는 길이라도 막상 외국인이 물어오면 머릿속이 복잡해지는 때가 있고 다양한 표현이 머리에 떠오르지 않는 경우도 있다. 그러므로 길을 묻거나 답하는 여러 가지 표현을 익혀두도록 하자.

Asking for Directions

Could you tell me how to get to (... the pool)?

How do I find (... StarBucks Coffee Shop)?

Pardon me, I'm lost, how do I get to the (... the main lobby)?

Which is the best route to (... Phuket Town)?

Could you direct me to (... the beach)?

Which way do I go to get to (... the hospital)?

Giving Directions

Take this passageway	Go up/down the steps
On your right/left	Turn right/left
Take the elevator	It's on the third floor
Follow this path	Turn right/left at the corridor
It's about 50 meters	Go above 3 kilometers
Cross the street	It's on your right/left

It's in the middle of the block　　It's on the corner

Drive south on 4233

It's next to　/　across from　/　between　/　in front of

Drive to Jackson street and turn left/right

Quiz

다음 대화에서 빈 칸에 들어갈 올바른 단어나 구는?

Mary Rogers : Hi, can I help you find something?

1. You : Yes, I'm looking for the Guggenheim Museum... but I think I'm
   _____.

   ① gone   ② confused   ③ lost

   Mary Rogers : Oh! I'm going to the Guggenheim Museum. I'll show you
                   where it is.

2. You : Thank you! I really _____ that.

   ① thank   ② appreciate   ③ approve

   Mary Rogers : My name is Mary, by the way. Where are you from?

3. You : I'm _____. My name is Adriana.

   ① from Italy   ② Italy   ③ from Italian

4. You : Pardon me, do you _____ Emilio's Restaurant is?

   ① recognize where   ② know where   ③ know some

   Person on Street : Emilio's.... Isn't that on Beverly?

5. You : I'm not sure. _____ it was around here.

① Someone told me　　② I said　　③ You can say

Person on Street : Yeah, I know the place.... It is on Beverly. OK, you have to turn around and drive that way... and when you get to Beverly Blvd, turn right.

6. You : So, I have to make a _____ and go back the other way?

① U-turnaround　　② U-turn　　③ U-maneuver

Person on Street : Yes, until you get to Beverly Blvd.

7. You : And how many _____ is that from here?

① blocks　　② squares　　③ stops

Person on Street : I'm not sure, but it's about 1 mile, more or less.

Vocabulary

1. passage-way = passageway, corridor, hall, way
2. walk-way = crosswalk
3. look for = search, find
4. turn left
5. turn right
6. make a U-turn
7. go straight

Answers

1. lost   2. appreciate   3. from Italy
4. know where   5. Someone told me   6. U-turnaround
7. blocks

런던에서 관광용어 배우기
(Travel Vocabulary in London)

Chapter 5

- 영화 '노팅힐(Notting Hill)' 관광

1. 대화(Target Language)

각 학문분야에 전공분야별 전문용어가 있듯이 관광산업에서 사용되는 영어표현 또한 단어가 가지는 사전적 의미 외에 다른 의미를 가진 경우가 하다하다. 그러므로 관광산업에서 주로 사용되는 영어표현을 익히는 것은 관광산업의 전문가로 일하는 경우 중요한 기초가 될 것이다.

Travel Vocabulary

Noun	Adjectives	Verbs
Accommodation	Adventurous	Sightsee
Attraction	Budget	Relax
Attraction	Breath-taking	Rest
Facilities	Coastal	Stroll
Itinerary	Cosmopolitan	Tour
Journey	Luxurious	Visit
Luggage	Mountainous	
Tourism	Peaceful	
Tourist	Picturesque	
Trip	Remote	
	Scenic	
	Traditional	

Idioms and Slang Terms We Might Use When Talking about Travel

모든 언어에는 마치 생명이 있는 것처럼 어느 때 새로운 단어가 태어나고 한창 쓰이다가 어느덧 거의 아무도 사용하지 않는 고어가 되어 사라져버리는 경우를 본다. 다음 어구들이 관광산업에서 어떤 의미로 통용되고 사용되고 있는지를 이해하여 잘 사용하길 바란다.

Travel bug － The urge to travel

Off the beaten track/path － a place where few people go, away from the frequently travelled routes.

Travel light － to bring very few things with you when you on a trip

To hit the road － to leave a place or begin a journey

Bright and early － very early in the morning

Conversation Questions about Travel 39(여행에 대한 질문들)

1. What are the main reasons people travel?

2. What are some benefits of travel?

3. Do you travel much within your country?

4. Have you travelled outside your country?

5. Where have you been?

6. What is the best place you have been to?

7. Do you have any current travel plans?

8. Could you live in another country for the rest of your life?

9. What was your best holiday you have ever had?

10. What is your worst travel experience?

11. Have you ever travelled on your own?

12. Do you prefer to travel on your own or with others?

13. What are your favourite types of vacations?

14. How are environmental problems changing the way people travel?

15. How does the recession affect people's travel plans?

16. What are the advantages and disadvantages of tourism?

17. Do you have a fear of flying?

18. Do you ever have to travel for business?

19. Do you prefer to travel by train, bus, plane or ship?

20. Have you ever been in a difficult situation while traveling?

21. How do you spend your time when you are on holiday and the weather is bad?

22. Do you like camping holidays?

23. Are there any countries that you would never like to visit? Why?

24. What are some things that you always take with you on a trip?

25. What countries would you like to visit? Why?

26. What's the most beautiful place you've ever been to?

27. When was the last time you travelled?

28. Where type of accommodation do you like to stay in when you travel, for example, hotel, cabin, tent, lodge?

29. Do you prefer to visit another country or travel within your own country?

30. Do you prefer to visit cities or more remote areas?

31. Do you like traveling to countries that have a different language from your own?

32. What types of leisure activities do you do on your holiday?

33. What are popular tourist destinations in your country?

34. Do you prefer active or relaxing holidays? Why?

35. Do you travel with a lot of baggage or do you like to travel light?

36. Do you prefer hot countries or cool countries when you go on holiday?

37. Who makes the decisions when your family decides to go on holiday?

38. Would you like to travel to space?

39. Can you think of any bad things about travelling?

🎬 영화 노팅힐(Notting Hill)

독신의 괴상한 친구 스파이크와 함께 살고 있는 그는 노팅힐 시장 한쪽 구석에 위치한 조그마한 여행서적 전문점을 운영하고 있다. 그에게는 미래에 대한 포부나 설계는 사치에 불과하다. 여느 때와 마찬가지로 무미건조한 하루를 보내고 있던 그는 세계적으로 유명한 인기 영화배우 안나 스콧이 그의 책방 문을 열고 들어와 책을 사서 나가자 잠깐 동안에 일어난 이 엄청난 사건에 어쩔 줄을 모른다. 몇 분 뒤 오렌지 주스를 사서 돌아오던 그는 길 모퉁이를 돌던 안나와 부딪쳐 그녀에게 주스를 쏟고 만다. 윌리엄은 근처에 있는 그의 집으로 그녀를 안내하여 씻고 옷을 갈아 입도록 한다. 그리고 헤어지기 전에 받은 그녀의 갑작스런 키스를 잊지 못한다.

그녀와의 멋진 만남을 꿈꾸며 촬영이 끝나길 기다리던 그는 그녀가 그와의 사랑을 달갑지 않게 말하는 것을 우연히 듣고 그녀를 잊기로 결심한다. 윌리엄을 찾아온 안나는 오해였음을 말하고 자신의 사랑을 고백하지만 윌리엄은 더 이상 그녀와의 차이를 극복할 자신이 없음을 말하고 그녀를 거절한다. 그러나 그녀가 영국을 떠나기 마지막 날 기자 회견장에 참석하고 있다는 소식을 들은 윌리엄은 자신의 사랑을 놓치지 않기 위해 회견장으로 달려가는데…

Asking Directions

Could you tell me how to get to Tower Bridge?

How do I find a loo near here?

Excuse me. I wonder if you tell me the way to Buckingham palace?

영화 속 대화

Keziah   : No thanks, I'm a fruitarian.

Max   : I didn't realize that.

William   : And, ahm : what exactly is a fruitarian?

Keziah   : We believe that fruits and vegetables have feeling so we think cooking is cruel. We only eat things that have actually fallen off a tree or bush - that are, in fact, dead already.

William   : Right. Right. Interesting stuff. So, these carrots....

Keziah   : Have been murdered, yes.

William   : Murdered? Poor carrots. How beastly!

2. 런던(London) 소개

You probably won't come to London to take pictures. The population tends to be reserved, the weather inhospitable, and many of the most famous attractions of the city, e.g., the world's best theater and music, are simply unsuited to photography.

On the other hand, if business or pleasure brings you to London, there is plenty to satisfy an itchy shutter release finger. If you've a special interest in architecture and are willing to pack a tripod and a perspective correction lens, you'll find that London contains some of the world's most varied building designs.

1) Starting Out on the River

Many of the most famous sights of London are spread along the banks of the River Thames (from the old Celtic word teme, meaning "river", named by the Romans in AD 43 when they established Londinium). These include the Houses of Parliament and Big Ben, just behind which is Westminster Abbey. You'll see

Christopher Wren's St. Paul's Cathedral, the Tower, Tower Bridge, a replica of Shakespeare's Globe Theater, and dozens of modern buildings.

Hop a boat up the river to Kew Gardens, browse around this extraordinary botanical garden, then take another boat to Greenwich and the Millennium Dome. Take ISO 400 film and a zoom lens that extends to at least 200mm (on a 35mm camera).

2) Christopher Wren

If you're passionate about architecture, it is worth touring the works of Christopher Wren (1632-1723), the leading restorer of London after the Great Fire. Wren's most famous work is St. Paul's cathedral but there are 30 others scattered around the city. To do the job properly, you'll probably want to bring a wide-angle perspective-correction lens (see the relevant section of "Building a 35mm SLR System"), though sadly I've not yet toted one to London myself.

If you climb to the top of St. Paul's, you'll also find that it makes a reasonable post for photography of the Thames and London rooftops.

3) People Looking at Animals

Don't forget that London has one of the world's best zoos, right downtown in Regent's Park. Go on a fine day and you'll be able to take great photos of people gawking at the animals.

4) People Looking at Art

Art museums throughout London ban or restrict photography. For photos of people interacting with art treasures, head to the British Museum. Photography and even flash photography are allowed but tripods are banned. In December 2000, the British Museum opened a new courtyard comprised of a modern roof over the old round reading

room. It is one of the more dramatic and successful pieces of new architecture in London. The museum is free and open 7 days a week.

5) People (Sort of) Running Around in Wigs

For photographs of lawyers walking around in wigs, get down to the streets around the Royal Courts of Justice in Holburn. From 9:30 to 4:30 pm you can attend a trial and watch the be-wigged barristers plead. A lot of important and photogenic old buildings surround the courts.

6) Photographic Exhibitions

Pick up a copy of Time Out (www.timeout.com) at a newsstand for full listings of photography shows at galleries and museums. The Photographer's Gallery, in two separate buildings near Leicester Square (5 and 8 Great Newport Street), usually has an interesting show. In one of their buildings they've got a nice bookshop and in the other a cafe. Around the corner on Charing Cross Road is a comprehensive specialty photography book shop : Zwemmer.

7) Skip the Royal Stuff

Unless you like to wait on lines and stand around in crowds, skip all the royal stuff in London. If you're wandering around the city and your route takes you past Buckingham Palace, great. But don't wait around for the changing of the guard or a glimpse of the royal family.

8) Shops and Photo Labs

Napoleon dismissed the English as "a nation of shopkeepers" and there is certainly little about London to contradict this characterization. What is most interesting about shopping

in London is the high proportion of specialty shops run either by or for obsessive eccentrics. There are shops that sell only umbrellas. Shops that sell only pipes (but not tobacco). Shops that sell only Leica cameras. Shops that sell only books about movies. Charing Cross Road and Bloomsbury are particularly interesting for browsing old books, new books, 18th and 19th century engravings, and literary effluvia.

다우닝 10번가

9) Hotels

If you need Internet connectivity from your room, you're out of luck! As far as I can tell, there aren't any hotels in London with 10 base-T jacks in the rooms. Like a Jaguar or Rolls-Royce, English hotels look wonderful but they aren't very practical in the modern business world.

London is very large and very neighborhoodish. Pick your preferred area first and then your hotel. My personal favorite area is in Soho near the theaters. A very nice small hotel is the Covent Garden at 10 Monmouth Street, phone (020) 7806 1000. Farther from the theaters but larger is the Savoy Hotel. The Savoy has history, views up the river, and a rooftop swimming pool. It was built in the late 1880s by Gilbert and Sullivan's business manager, Richard D'Oyly Carte.

I've stayed at "MyHotel" in Bloomsbury. For $300 per night I got a stylishly decorated room about 1 meter larger all around than the bed. There was no minibar in my room but the bathroom was unheated and quite cold enough to use as a fridge for cold drinks bought from the convenience store around the corner.

Despite double windows the noise from the busy street below was loud enough to require earplugs at night. And when I woke up in the middle of the night and wanted to surf the Internet, I just put on some clothes. There was no in-room Ethernet but across the street is an easyEverything 24-hour Internet cafe.

10) Restaurants

The Michelin Red Guides are the most reliable source for restaurants throughout Europe. If you care about food, you'll definitely want the Michelin Red Guide London. Indian and Asian food in London tends to be quite good. There is a Chinatown area around Gerrard Street just north of the National Gallery where you can get a dim sum lunch seven days a week.

Among the fast food chains, Pret a Manger chain is my favorite, with clean and simple sandwiches and salads.

11) Guidebooks

Dorling Kindersley's Eyewitness London is the most useful guidebook, especially for a photographer, because the book contains a small snapshot of each site. Thus you're able to make an informed decision as to whether or not the journey will be photographically worthwhile. The Dorling Kindersley guide is also good about indicating whether or not photography is allowed within a site. Finally, the guide contains a London Underground map on the back cover, a small street atlas, restaurant recommendations, and hotel listings.

12) Getting There

Most international nonstops fly into Heathrow (LHR). Traffic from Heathrow into downtown London goes over the insanely busy M4 highway. If you've arrived during the morning rush hour, it may be much faster to take the London Underground, which stops right in the terminals (40 minutes to downtown), or the Heathrow Express train (15 minutes to Paddington Station). Try to avoid Gatwick (LGW) airport, which is twice as far from central London as Heathrow.

For airline choices, see the photo.net guide to international airlines. Bottom line : British Airways is most likely to have a nonstop flight from wherever you are and happens to be as good as it gets in the airline business.

13) Getting Around

Taxis in London can be expensive. Rates are high and the distances are vast. On the plus side, every driver of a London black cab will know every street in the city. The Underground covers the city very thoroughly, is fast and runs every few minutes at peak times. For scenery on a budget, hop a London bus (the driver will give you change!). The bus will be your only option after midnight when the Underground shuts down.

14) Survival

American citizens don't need a visa to visit England.

The time in London is GMT, i.e., five hours ahead of New York. Thus if it is 9:00 am in New York, it is already 2:00 pm in London.

Electricity in England is 240V at 50 Hz. Most laptop computer and digital camera power supplies can function on this power and at most you'll need a mechanical adaptor. Business hotel rooms often are equipped with an American-style plug near the desk. If not, the hotel will lend you an adapter.

15) Going Beyond

Many of England best sights are within a two-hour drive of London. The Roman city of Bath, just to the west, makes a good base for exploring Stonehenge, Salisbury Cathedral, and a variety of rural hamlets. In the summer, a one-hour train ride south to Brighton is worthwhile for photographs of English seaside tack. You won't need a car to explore the waterfront. Both Cambridge and Oxford are close to London. If you have to pick one for a photography excursion, Cambridge is probably the better choice.

British Rail can take you directly to most towns in England but for photographing the countryside, you're much better off renting a car. Driving in London itself can be intimidating. You might be better off taking the Heathrow Express to the airport and picking up your car there.

3. 상황별 대화(Conversation by Situation)

At the Hotel : Talking about What You Like/Don't Like - 호텔 내에서 사용하는 여러 가지 표현

1) I love this room. It's very pretty!

2) I don't like this room. It's filthy!

3) I love this view. It's really beautiful!

4) I like this restaurant. The food is very tasty.

5) I don't like the way he behaves. He's very rude!

6) I love the service here. It's very professional.

7) I'll pass on (=I won't take) the room. It's too noisy.

8) I'll pass on (=I won't take) the room. It's a little too expensive.

9) I don't like this room. It doesn't seem safe.

10) I really like this room. It's very cozy.

At the Restaurant : Talking about What You Like/Don't Like - 레스토랑에서 사용하는 여러 가지 표현

1) I love this meal. It's very tasty!

2) I don't eat meat. I'm a vegetarian.

3) I can't eat greasy/fatty food. I'm on a diet.

4) I love simple food, but my husband likes bland food.

5) This meal is fantastic! My compliments to the chef.

6) I love the service here. It's very professional.

7) This restaurant is too noisy. I'm looking for somewhere more quiet.

8) That was perfect! I'm full.

9) I want to order something else. I'm still hungry.

10) That was a great meal! I thought the fish was prepared perfectly.

Shopping/Buying Things : Name the Item in the Picture - 쇼핑할 때 사용하는 여러 가지 표현

1. I am looking for a jacket .

2. These gloves are on sale.

3. This skirt is too short.

4. These jeans fit me well.

5. I need a new baseball cap .

6. This t-shirt is too big.

7. Do you sell boots ?

Quiz

다음 문장을 완성시키기에 적합한 단어를 박스 안 단어에서 골라 기입하세요.

gate / bottle / pass / cellphone / wallet / delayed / money / flight / bags / page

1. I lost my _____ and all my money was inside it.

2. I missed my _____.

3. I can't find my husband. Can you _____ him?

4. I can't find my departure _____.

5. The airline lost one of my _____.

6. I don't have enough _____ to buy a sandwich.

7. They won't let me take my _____ of water on the plane.

8. I lost my boarding _____.

9. My flight has been _____ for three hours.

10. Is there a public phone here? My _____ isn't working.

Vocabulary

1 itinerary = schedule

2. Travel light = to bring very few things with you when you on a trip

3. To hit the road = to leave a place or begin a journey

4. filthy = dirty

5. cozy = soft and comfortable

6. bland = plain, simple food

7. compliments = appreciation, thanks

8. complimentary = free, complementary = supplementary

Answers

1. wallet	2. flight	3. page
4. gate	5. bags	6. money
7. bottle	8. pass	9. delayed
10. cellphone		

베트남에서 쇼핑하기
(Shopping in Vietnam)

Chapter **6**

- 영화 '그린 파파야 향기(The Scent of Green Papaya)' 관광

1. 대화(Target Language)

관광에서 빠질 수 없는 즐거움 중 하나는 쇼핑이다. 귀국 전 공항 면세점에서 하는 쇼핑보다 여행지에서 전통시장을 찾아 그곳의 특색을 잘 살린 기념품을 사기도 하고 최근에는 여행 전에 이미 온라인을 통해 품목을 정해서 구매를 결정하는 경우가 증가하고 있다. 옷을 살 경우 사이즈에 대한 표현과 현지 화폐의 환율 등에 대한 표현 및 여행지에서 현금, 카드, 여행자수표 등을 가지고 다양한 방법으로 계산할 것에 대비한 표현을 익혀두자.

Staff : Welcome to the Boutique. How may I help you?

Guest : I'm looking for a bathing suit?

Staff : A one piece, two piece, or a bikini?

Guest : A two piece, but not too revealing.

Staff : We have some over here.

Guest : That blue and white dot one looks nice. How much is it?

Staff : It's 575 VND.

Guest : That's a bit pricey, but I'll take it.

Staff : Good afternoon, may I be of assistance?

Guest : Yes, how much is the carved elephant?

Staff : That's 755 VND.

Guest : Could you tell me what it's made from?

Staff : That's made from teak.

Guest : I'll take it.

Guest : Excuse me, do you have any yellow T-shirts?

Staff : Yes Sir, they are right over there.

Guest : Thanks. Do you have any bigger ones?

Staff : Let me check in the back. I'll return in a moment.

Guest : Thanks.

Staff : Good afternoon, may I be of assistance?

Guest : No thanks, just looking around.

Staff : OK, if you need anything, just let me know.

Guest : Oh, I will.

🎬 그린 파파야 향기 베트남 사이공 관광

1993년 칸 황금카메라상을 받은 이 영화의 줄거리
이다. 1951년 늦은 밤, 사이공의 어느 골목에 나타난
허름한 옷차림의 한 소녀가 골목길 주변을 두리번거
린다. 그 소녀가 찾는 곳은 자신이 식모살이를 할 주
인집이다. 소녀의 이름은 무이, 나이는 10살이며 3년
전 아버지가 죽고 엄마, 여동생과 살다가 가난한 가정
형편으로 어린 나이에 식모살이를 위해 이곳 사이공
까지 하루 종일 걸어서 도착하여 주인집에서 운영하
는 포목점을 겨우 찾아낼 수 있었다. 주인마님은 자신
의 남편에게 새로 온 식모 무이에 대해 얘기하지만 남

편은 무심한 표정으로 베트남 전통악기인 단 응우웬(Dan Nguyet)을 연주하느라 여념
이 없다.

주인집은 주인아저씨와 그의 부인인 마님과 주인아저씨의 어머니인 노마할머니 그
리고 장성한 큰아들 드렁, 무이보다 나이가 약간 더 많은 둘째 아들 램, 무이보다 나이
가 어린 막내 아들 틴이 한가족이며 무이는 오랫동안 이 집안에서 하녀로 일해 온 중년
의 아줌마와 같은 방을 쓴다. 빨래와 집안청소 일을 하며 음식 만들기도 배우는 무이에
게 철없는 막내 아들인 틴이 짓궂은 장난을 많이 치지만 무이와 같은 나이의 딸을 잃은
마님은 겉으로 드러내지 않지만 무이를 딸처럼 잘 대해준다. 어린 무이에게 3개월이
지나면 집에 가서 어머니를 만나고 올 수 있게 해준다고 말한다. 무이는 주인집에 놀러
온 큰 도련님의 친구 쿠옌을 보고 호감을 느낀다. 하녀 아줌마에게 쿠옌에 대해서 넌지
시 물어보며 마음속에 호감을 담아둔다.

Asking for Directions

Could you tell me how to get to the sea coast?

How do I find the way to the shopping mall?

Pardon me, I'm lost, how do I get to the tourist information?

영화 속 대화

Mui : In our garden, there are many green papaya trees with lots of fruit. Papaya fruits which are well ripen colours light yellow and taste sweet just like sugar.

Cuen's Fiance : How many Vietnam women pat her fiance's head? Mom said it was strict in the past. They had been expelled when touched man's head.

2. 베트남(Vietnam) 소개

Vietnam is a country full of photographic opportunities. The landscape is diverse and includes a very long and beautiful coastline, karstic rock formations, and mountains. Because Vietnam is just doing its first steps in the modern world (unlike Thailand or China which are much more developed) there are still plenty of opportunities to observe traditional lifestyles and traditions.

People have an amazing ethnic diversity and most like to be photographed. There is also interesting architecture all around the country, although it is not as spectacular as in other countries of South-East Asia such as Cambodia or Myanmar.

Now is a good time to visit Vietnam. Vietnam opened itself to tourism in the late 80s. At the beginning there were still a lot of red tape and travel restrictions, and the tourist infrastructure was quite poor. In the late 90s I found it easy to travel in Vietnam.

The country is industrializing extremely

quickly to meet the needs of its dense population. Things are changing very fast, in a few years, the traditional way of life might be gone, and uncontrolled development might have spoiled some of the finest scenery.

1) A Few Highlights

In any town, the market would be a good place to start for street photography. In particular the Cholon (the Ho Chi Minh City's Chinatown) markets are particularly lively. There are wholesale markets there which are very interesting to see.

In general, the smaller the town, the more authentic the atmosphere will be. The rural lifestyle hasn't changed much in centuries. One of the most interesting sights in the Delta are the floating markets and associated river life. Near Can Tho, there are three different floating markets.

Although they are well-known, the level of "commercialization" is still considerably less than the floating markets of Thailand. Often you won't see other travellers on the water at all. Often, the North will be more authentic, but more reserved, less open and welcoming at first.

You will find in the far north mountains the highest concentration of well-preserved hill-tribe culture. The Sapa market now is visited by almost as many tourists as local people, but others, such as the markets around Bac Ha, are still very authentic and would be a unique experience.

Most of the hill-tribe people don't mind the camera, however, there are some ethnic groups which are camera-shy, such as the Dzao. Don't harass them.

2) Architecture

In the center, most of the city of Hoi An has well preserved ancient homes. In that area, there are some interesting Cham archeological sites, and the Danang's

marble mountains have some of the finest troglodyte sanctuaries I have ever seen. The imperial citadel of Hue used to rival Beijing's forbidden city, but most of it was destroyed during the Tet offensive in 1968. However the imperial mausoleums spread along the Perfume river are well preserved.

Besides communist monuments (and one of the only remaining Lenin statues), Hanoi and its surrounding have numerous ancient temples, especially near Ninh Binh, where you'll also find an interesting church built in local style. Hanoi itself has the nostalgia of a fading postcard of colonial French architecture. The stained and aging painted walls have a lot of character.

3) Landscapes

The delta being quite flat, most of the interesting landscapes there will be on the coast, especially near the Cambodia border where it gets more mountainous. The central portion of the cost is beautiful, with the mountains dropping into the South China Sea. The road between Da Nang and Hue is particularly scenic.

There are remarkable karstic formations in the North, comparable to some the better known sites of South China. The site of Halong Bay is deservedly famous, but it can be challenging to get a good picture there.

The site of Tam Coc has similarly shaped rocks, but instead of being in the sea, they are among cultivated rice fields. The most beautiful and wild mountain scenery are in the far north regions near the China border.

4) How to Travel

For most independent travelers, the cheapest and most convenient way to see a lot of the country is to use local budget travel agencies (such as Cafe Sinh). However, if you are serious about photography, I would recommend that you avoid using those tours.

They try to pack a lot of travel into a relatively short time, and you'll find that being in a group will not leave you the freedom you need to explore and be in the right place at the right time.

A better alternative would be to travel from one city to another on public or private bus system, and then spend time on your own exploring the cities. The drawback is that you will see plenty of interesting rural scenes while riding on a very slow (by occidental standards) bus, and you will wish you could get out. It's pretty difficult to get a decent photo from a bus window while the bus is bouncing around.

The best solution is to rent a car and driver. The driver comes for free as you're mostly paying for the vehicle and mileage, at rates which locally look exorbitant but are actually comparable to those found in the West. He sometimes can serve as your guide, helping with lodging and meal arrangements, as well as facilitating your communication with the locals.

It is a good idea to try to go on a shorter trip with him before committing to hire him for the whole length of your trip. Many drivers do not speak English, in which case you will also need a guide/interpret. As a foreigner, you are not permitted to drive a vehicle in Vietnam, and you will soon realize that there is a good reason for that.

There are also a number of places where you'll be traveling on water (the Delta, Nha Trang, Halong, the Perfume river...). Consider renting your own boat for the same reasons as above. It's not so expensive.

When you are staying in a large city, a car is not necessary. Instead, what I like to do is to ride on the back of a moto-taxi. This is fairly inexpensive, and fast, and makes it easy to stop when you want. Cyclos are a good option too if you have time, since you can photograph from them. Ask your hotel/guesthouse manager to recommend you someone to take you for a ride, rather than picking someone at random. You'll get more dependable and safe service this way.

5) Local Conditions

You might think that because this is the tropics, there is plenty of light, but don't make the mistake of bringing only slow film. Because the sun there is so high, even more than anywhere else, on sunny days the only nice light appears early in the morning and late in the afternoon, so you'll be facing reduced levels.

Because of the ever present atmospheric haze, sunsets and sunrises give a very warm and soft light which is particularly beautiful. During midday, most people take refuge in the shade (not that you'd like to shoot portraits in the harsh light anyways), where it can gets fairly dark. In the North, it often gets overcast while the South is sunny and hot. You will need fairly fast film or lenses.

Typically (except for a few months) day time temperature is about 90 F with high humidity. It will be pretty tiring to walk around, so it would help not to carry a ton of gear.

6) Film

You can find locally cheap negative film. On the other hand, if you are shooting slide film or B&W, better bring everything you will need with you. Those two kinds of film are pretty rare. The problem is that often film have been stocked for a long time in hot conditions. Fuji film can probably be found only in a few stores in Ho Chi Minh city and one store in Hanoi.

I can make only recommendations for slide film, as I use only occasionally other types. For general purpose use, I like Fuji Astia/Sensia II. The usable dynamic range is better than most slide films due to the lower contrast, and the skin tones are very natural.

Velvia is great for scenics in good light, or under overcast conditions (where a tripod might be necessary). If you find that under overcast skies, Astia tends to be a bit dull, you can try Kodak E 100 VS, which gives you color characteristics quite close to Velvia, but with an extra stop. Think also about packing some film for use at 200 or even 400 ASA.

7) Cameras and Lenses

You won't need long telephoto lenses. Distant views tend to be too hazy, and people are approachable. The longest I had is a 200 and this was plenty. On the other hand, street scenes tend to get crowded, and you will often get close to your subjects, so having at least a 28 is a must. What I found with Astia is that at mid day, in the shade, the exposure was very often between 1/15 and 1/60 at f4. This means that if you are using a consumer zoom, you won't have enough light to hand-hold and get a sharp image.

You could forego the convenience of zooms, and go with a few primes, or carry a big f2.8 zoom. If you do so, you might find that the depth of field is too small for some subjects (like the vendor standing in front of a stand of interesting tropical fruits). Personally I have found the 28-135 IS lens from Canon to be extremely practical.

would solve any problems. There might be older machines hanging around in smaller airports, although at the Hue airport they didn't have any at all!

8) Photographic Restrictions

Do not photograph anything which might be military sensitive, or police doing their duty if you don't want to risk your film confiscated. Once in the mountains I was photographing scenery, and a plain clothes policeman came and harassed me, claiming that I was photographing a bridge.

Explaining Safety, Rules and Etiquette - English for Tour Guides

This page covers vocabulary needed by people working as tour guides in an English-speaking context.

When giving a tour there may be rules and safety precautions that you need to explain. It is best if you memorize a speech rather than read from a card.

People will pay more attention to you and understand you more clearly if you look into their eyes as you speak. After you have explained the rules and safety precautions make sure that guests have understood you, by asking, "Are there any questions about this?" or "Is everyone clear on the rules?".

Also, tourists will appreciate any helpful advice you can give them, such as where to exchange their money, what types of transportation to use, and how to obey the traffic rules. Finally, if there are any customs or matters of etiquette that you think tourists should be aware of, this is a good time to let them know.

9) Explaining Rules

Tour Guide

- You are strictly forbidden from taking photographs inside the museum.
- Please stay on the marked path.
- I'm sure this goes unsaid, but remember to place all trash in the garbage bins.
- Please pay attention to the time. We don't want to keep the driver waiting.
- Classes are in session, so we need to keep our voices down.
- The bus will be leaving at 5:00 pm sharp.
- You'll have some free time to look around after lunch.
- Please meet back here in one hour.

10) Explaining Safety

Tour Guide

- Please keep your seatbelt fastened at all times.
- I ask that you keep your hands inside the train.
- As a safety precaution, please stand behind the yellow line.
- For your own safety, we ask that you refrain from putting your arms out the window.
- Please do not feed the animals.

- Please remain seated until we come to a full stop.
- Please stay with your group at all times.
- Please keep to the sidewalk.
- I do not recommend swimming here. The water is very rough.
- We suggest only carrying small amounts of cash.
- These rules are for your own comfort and safety.

11) Explaining Etiquette and Customs

Tour Guide

- It is customary in our country to tip the friendly bus driver.
- In this region we bow rather than shake hands during a first meeting.
- Though the all-inclusive includes tips for the servers, it does not include tips for the bellboy.
- To indicate that you want to get on or off the bus simply wave your hand at the driver.

3. 상황별 대화(Conversation by Situation)

Shopping/Buying Things - 쇼핑센터에서 사용하는 표현

May (can) I be of assistance?

How much are the... (blue jeans)?

How can (may) I help you?

Could you tell me the price of that... (camera)?

May I assist you?

Do you have any... (playing cards)?

Could I help you find something?   No thanks, I'm just browsing.

How much is this cap?   That's... ($9.99).

How much are these earrings?   They are... (4500 Baht).

What... (size do you need)?   I... (wear a size 12).

I'm sorry, that's the largest size we carry.

Do you have this in... (a larger size)?

Yes, it also comes in... (green, red, and blue).

Does this come in... (a different color)?

Shopping 1 : General - 드레스의 사이즈와 색상을 고르며 입어보는 상황

Clerk : Can I help you find something?

You : Yes, do you have this dress in a bigger size?

Clerk : What size are you looking for?

You : Size 6... But if you have a size 8, I'll try it on as well.

Clerk : OK, let me check in the back.... (Comes Back) There you go.... I
       found the dress in a size 8....

You : Thanks. Where are your fitting rooms?

Clerk : Just around the corner.... Let me know if you need anything else.

(You Try on the Dress)

Clerk : So how did that fit?

Clerk : Not too good.... I think I need a smaller size.

Clerk : That's the smallest size we have in that color.... Would you like me
       to look for another color?

You : No, I like this color.... Thanks anyway.

Shopping 2 : General - 스카프와 장갑을 사는 상황

Store Clerk : Can I help you find something?

You   : Yes, does this scarf come in yellow?

Store Clerk : No we don't have it in yellow... only in black, red, and orange.

You   : Oh, OK. And it's on sale right?

Store Clerk : Yes, it is. All our scarves and hats are 20% off today and tomorrow.

You : And what about the gloves?

Store Clerk : They're normal price.

You : These gloves don't have a price tag. How much are they?

Store Clerk : Those are... $15.99.

You : OK, I'll take them. Could you wrap them up for me? They're a present.

Shopping 3 : Postcards, Souvenirs - 기념품을 사는 상황

You : How much are these postcards?

Clerk : They're 5 for $2.

You : I only need two.

Clerk : If you buy them individually, they're $0.50 each.

You : OK. I'll take these two. Do you sell any souvenirs here?

Clerk : Yes, we do. We've got some mugs, fridge magnets, and more... they're right over there. Is there anything in particular you're looking for?

You : Yes, my mother collects plates with names of cities. Do you have any?

Clerk : Hmm... no, we don't. But there's a store just down the street that sells those.

You : What's the name of that store?

Clerk : It's called "Empire State Souvenirs". It's just down the street to your right.

Quiz

다음 대화에서 빈 칸에 들어갈 올바른 단어나 구는?

Store Clerk : Can I help you find something?

1. You : Yes, does this scarf _____ in yellow?

① arrive   ② have   ③ come

Store Clerk : No we don't have it in yellow... only in black, red, and orange.

2. You : Oh, OK. And it's _____, right?

① being sold   ② on sale   ③ on discount

Store Clerk : Yes, it is. All our scarves and hats are 20% off today and tomorrow.

3. You : And _____ the gloves?

① what   ② what if   ③ what about

Store Clerk : They're normal price.

Vocabulary

1. reveal = expose, make public

2. pricey = expensive

3. try on = wear, put on

4. VND = Vietnames ngàn đồng, Vietnames money

Answers

1. come   2. on sale   3. what about

Chapter 7

일본에서 관광가이드 영어하기
(Tour Guide English in Japan)

- 영화 '러브레터(Love Letter)' 관광

1. 대화(Target Language)

  여행은 즐거움을 우선 목표로 출발한다. 하지만 휴가가 아니라 여행 인솔자(이하 가이드)로서 여러 명을 안내하여 여행할 경우 인솔자는 시간과의 전쟁을 치러야 할 것이다. 모든 일정이 정해진 시간 내에 일사천리로 진행되어야 할 것이며 신속 정확을 위해 가이드가 사용하는 언어는 표준화되고 알아듣기 쉬운 영어가 되는 것이 중요하다. 본 장에서는 가이드에게 필요한 다양한 표현을 익힐 수 있도록 준비하였다.

Guide : It's about a three minute ride up to the top of the mountain. As we pass the two towers the gondolla may sway a little.

Man : This thing is safe, right?

Guide : Yes, you don't have anything to worry about. We do about 100 trips a day up the mountain, and these tours have been going on for over ten years without any accidents. Keep your eyes open for wildlife as we ascend. It isn't uncommon to see deer and even bears.

Woman: What's that mountain to the left called?

Guide : That's Mount Karen. And to the right of that with the three small points is Mount Brown. Now, if you look up straight ahead, you should be able to see a large eagle's nest. Does everyone see it there?

Man : Are there any baby birds?

Guide : That's a good question. I haven't seen any yet, but we usually see them around this time of year.

Woman: What's that lake down there, to the right of the green meadow?

Guide : I'm glad you asked. That's John Lake. It's actually a man made pond that was built as part of a conservation effort over twenty years ago. During the 70's there was a lot of clearcutting of forests in the area, and much of the wildlife was lost. Since John Lake was built, ducks, swans, and geese have returned to the area.

Man : Is this the highest mountain in this region?

Guide : No, actually, Mount Heather, which you we will be able to see in just a minute or so has the highest peak. But, this is the highest mountain for recreational purposes like skiing and guided tours.

Woman: Can you ski throughout the year?

Guide : No, it warms up enough to actually suntan up there in the summer. Oh, look everyone. There are two deer feeding in the clearing right below us.

Man : Thanks, that should be a great photo. So... what is there to do besides ski at the top of the hill at this time of year?

Guide : Oh, there's plenty to do. We have horseback riding, snowmobile tours, and a petting zoo for children. If you look to your left you'll see the snowmobile trail going through the mountain.

🎞 영화 러브레터(Love Letter)

사랑했던 연인 후지이 이쓰키가 죽은 지 2년. 그의 약혼녀 와타나베 히로코(나카야마 미호)는 여전히 그를 잊지 못하고 있다. 추모식 날, 히로코는 그의 중학교 졸업 앨범에서 지금은 사라진 그의 옛 주소를 발견하고 그리운 마음에 안부를 묻는 편지를 띄운다. 하지만 며칠 후, 후지이 이쓰키로부터 거짓말처럼 답장이 날아오고, 히로코는 편지를 보낸 그 사람이 그와 같은 이름을 지닌 여자이며 그의 중학교 동창이라는 사실을 알게 되는데…

Asking for Directions

Can you tell me how to get to the sushi house?
How do I find the train station to Narita airport?
Pardon me, I'm lost, how do I get to the post office?

영화 속 대화

Hiroko : Guess what? I wrote a letter and mailed it to that address.

Man : The address doesn't exist anymore as you see.

Hiroko : I see. It's a letter to Heaven.

Man : You're really full of surprises.

Hiroko : But... guess what happened?.... I got a reply.

Man : From heaven? You must be kidding.

Hiroko : Here you are.
He says "Dear Watanabe Hiroko, I'm basically fine... but I now have a cold. From Fujii Itsuki." Isn't this strange?

2. 일본(Japan) 소개

Imagine a country where everyone is good at his or her job.

Imagine a country where everyone has respect for elders and teachers. Imagine a country where every shop clerk treats each customer like an honored guest.

Imagine a country where everyone wears expensive clothing, the food is slurpy, and there aren't any napkins because apparently nobody needs them. Imagine a country where everyone has good taste.

One thing that is tough for an American to understand is how Tokyo-centric Japan is. In the U.S., if you are ambitious for money you move to New York. If you are ambitious for power you move to Washington, DC. Those who want to get into show business move to Los Angeles.

Techies move to Silicon Valley. People who love knowledge and learning move to Boston. In Japan, each of these types of people would move to Tokyo. And they have! Tokyo is corporate headquarters. Tokyo has the best universities.

Tokyo is the seat of Japan's powerful central government. The good thing about Tokyo-centricity is that a Japanese family can stay together even if the members develop divergent interests.

The bad thing is that real estate prices are insane, commuting means 75 minutes standing on a packed train, and one is constantly part of a crowd. As a tourist, it is a marvel to see how well Tokyo functions despite the crowds. In planning your trip remember that you can escape those crowds merely by leaving Tokyo.

1) General Tips

The best months to visit Japan are spring and fall. The climate in Tokyo is similar to that of New York City. You can control the climate to some extent by traveling up into the mountains, north to Hokkaido, or south to subtropical Okinawa. If possible, I recommend starting your trip in a part of Japan that is smaller and slower-paced than Tokyo. Nara and Kyoto are reasonable choices, served by the Kansai international airport.

With its mountains, oceans, and spectacular urbanscapes, Japan is too varied to make any general film recommendations. Check the photo.net film page for our latest thinking.

The Japanese are incredibly friendly to photographers. Some museums and temples restrict the use of tripods but otherwise this is a place where you can snap away in comfort. Street photography is easy despite the language barrier; the Japanese are especially tolerant of foreigners.

It is easy to buy a camera or film in Japan but don't expect bargains on most items. Generic 35mm gear is about the same price as in New York. Certain kinds of medium-format cameras, such as Mamiya, can be substantially cheaper in Japan.

2) Survival

If you're from most Western countries, you don't need a visa to enter Japan

for 90 days.

You will most likely be flying into either Narita Airport (near Tokyo) or Kansai (near Osaka and the airport of choice for visiting Kyoto and Nara). If you've traveled light, you can take a train from Narita into Tokyo. If you've got a lot of luggage and are staying at a big hotel, take the special airport bus (90 minutes). If you come into Kansai and are going to Kyoto, the train is the only reasonable option.

Considering that English is a required subject in Japanese government schools, it is remarkable how few Japanese speak English. Remember also that you won't be able to read most signs or product packaging. Prepare to be disoriented and confused.

You'll have to try very hard to get food poisoning in Japan. The guidebooks caution only against raw bear meat and raw wild boar due to risk of trichinosis.

Electric power is 100V (US voltage is about 117) and plugs are American-style two-prong affairs. Curiously, the line frequency is 50 Hz in Tokyo and eastern Japan, 60 Hz in the west. Most laptop and digital camera power supplies will work fine in Japan.

The currency in Japan is the Yen. You get about 100 of these to the dollar (check Yahoo! Finance for the latest rates). Bring lots of US dollars in cash or travelers checks into Japan and also try to use the ATMs in the airport or the post office.

The average bank ATM will not work with an American bank or credit card! Remember that, at least as of September 2000, Japan remains a cash-oriented society. Six of us ate a $1000 sushi meal. We had to pay in cash. We visited a rare book and print shop. They had some lovely drawings of koi for $2000. Cash only.

Japan is about as safe and crime-free as a country with 125 million people can be. My friend Curt left his Nikon FM2 on a subway train. He complained about the loss to a Japanese friend who asked "Why didn't you go to the lost and found and get it back?" It did not occur to the Japanese that the camera would have been misappropriated; it did not occur to the American that the $500 camera would be returned. Curt went to the lost and found. The Nikon was there.

Bring your familiar over-the-counter medicines with you. The Japanese do not have a strong tradition of self-care. If you're sick, you go to the doctor and take whatever is prescribed without asking what it is. Pharmacists are helpful but some of your favorite drugs may not exist, e.g., Sudafed, unless you go to the American Pharmacy (Tokyo : (03) 3271-4034).

3) Getting Around

Traveling by train is very practical. Check the travel planner at www.businessinsightjapan.com for schedules and fares.

Showing Places of Interest - English for Tour Guides

This page covers vocabulary needed by people working as tour guides in an English-speaking context.

Silence can be uncomfortable during a tour. While you can't talk the whole time, you should try to know as much about the history, scenery, and culture (in English) for the places where you are giving tours so that you can keep the tourists interested.

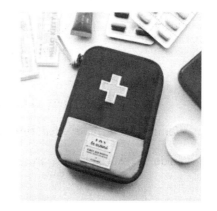

If you ever run out of something to say, you can always point out something such as a landmark or a type of tree or flower. Here are some different ways you can point out interest points during the tour.

3. 상황별 대화(Conversation by Situation)

Asking to the Guide 1 - 가이드가 단체 여행자의 질문에 답하는 상황

Guide : If you have any questions while we're going along, please don't hesitate to ask.

Man : I have a question actually.

Guide : Sure, what's that?

Man : Where's the best place to have dinner around here?

Guide : Well, that's a tough question. There are so many good restaurants. My personal favourite is Spaghetti Alley.

Man : How do we get there?

Guide : I'll point it out when we pass it. It's going to come up on your right in a few minutes.

Woman : My daughter wants to know if we're going to be passing any castles today?

Guide : Castles. No I'm afraid all of the castles are further into the city. We're going to be staying near the coast today. I can give you a map of the city, though. It shows where all of the castles are.

Man : Sorry, I have another question.

Guide : No problem. That's what I'm here for.

Man : Are we allowed to take pictures once we get inside the museum?

Guide : Oh, I'm glad you asked that. I forgot to mention that taking photographs inside the art gallery and the museum is prohibited. However, you can take pictures of the grounds and the outside of the buildings. The architecture is beautiful.

Woman : Oh, and what time will we be stopping for lunch?

Guide : We'll break around noon and meet back at the bus at 12:45 sharp.

Asking to the Guide 2 - 갑작스런 투어 취소 발생에 처한 가이드의 상황

You : Does the sightseeing tour leave from here?

Other Tourist : Yes, I think so. We're just waiting for the tour guide to arrive.

You : Isn't the tour supposed to start at 4:30?

Other Tourist : Yes, it is. I guess the tour guide is running a little late....

(5 Minutes Later)

Tour Guide : I'm sorry everyone, the 4:30 pm tour has been cancelled. We're having some mechanical problems with our bus.

You : So there won't be any more tours today?

Tour Guide : I'm not sure right now. We'll have to wait and see....

You : How long do we have to wait?

Tour Guide : I'm not sure. They're fixing the bus right now. If they don't fix it in 30 minutes, I'll give all of you your money back.

You : And how long does the last tour once it starts?

Tour Guide : About one hour.

Sightseeing : At the Museum - 박물관 관람 관련 문의

You : Hello. What time does the museum close today?

Museum Worker : The museum closes at 7:00 pm.

You : And what time does it open tomorrow?

Museum Worker : The museum opens at 9:00 am.

You : And how much is the admission?

Museum Worker : The admission fee is $8... $5 if you're a student.

You : And are there any special exhibitions on(=happening) right now?

Museum Worker : Yes, there's a special exhibition of Edward Hopper's early paintings.

You   : Is this included in the price of admission?

Museum Worker : No, there's a separate $5 charge for the exhibition.

Tour Guide 1 - 가이드가 관광지를 설명할 때 필요한 다양한 표현

단체여행객들 앞에서 가이드는 손으로 방향을 가리키며 설명을 한다.

자, 여러분 앞에/우측에/좌측에/위로/저 코너를 돌면/멀리서…

- In front of you is...

- On your right/left you will see...

- Up ahead...

- On your left you will see...

- As we turn the corner here, you will see...

- In the distance...

- If you look up you will notice...

- Off to the north...

- Look to the east...

- To your west...

버스로 이동 시… "잠시 후 우리는 OOO을 지나가게 될 것입니다.…"

- In a few minutes we'll be passing...

걷다가 지친 일행에게 용기를 주며… "자, 이제 OOO에 거의 이르렀습니다."

- We are now coming up to...

- As you will see...

여러분이 알아차렸겠지만…

- You may have noticed...

여러분, 잘 보세요.…

● Take a good look at...

제가 강조하고 싶은 것은…

● I'd like to point out...

자, 눈을 크게 뜨고 OOO을 보세요.

● Keep your eyes open for...

Tour Guide 2 - 가이드가 문의에 답할 때 사용하는 표현

질문 있나요?

● Do you have a question, Sir?
● Yes? (if you see a hand raised)

제가 뭔가 도와드릴 일이 있을까요?

● Is there something I can help you with?
● I'll try my best to answer your questions.
● I'm afraid I don't have the answer to that. (Sorry I don't know.)

여행 중 일행에게서 답하기 곤란한 질문을 받을 경우에 대처하는 재미난 영어표현

● That's an interesting question.
● I wish I knew the answer. (Sorry, I don't know.)
● Hmm. That's a tough (difficult) question.
● I'll have to look into that further.
● I'll have to ask someone about that.
● Hmm. I've never been asked that before.
● Pardon my English; I don't quite understand your question.
● I'm not sure, but I can find out for you.

Health : Seeing a Doctor - 여행 중 현지 의사에게 진찰받는 상황

Doctor : What seems to be the problem?

You : I haven't been feeling well.... I have been throwing up(=vomiting) for the past 12 hours.

Doctor : I see.... And do you have a fever?

You : Yes, I checked my temperature two hours ago. It was 101 (38.5c.).

Doctor : Hmmm.... Sounds like you got food poisoning. Does your body feel sore?

You : Yes, my body does hurt a little.

Doctor : OK. I'm going to prescribe an antibiotic... Penicillin....

You : I'm allergic to Penicillin.... Could you prescribe another one?

Doctor : Oh, OK. I'll prescribe another one.... Take one pill every six hours, drink plenty of water, and stay in bed for the next 24 hours.

You : Thank you, doctor! Where can I buy these pills?

Doctor : There's a pharmacy right next to the clinic.

Health - 여행 중 몸이 아플 경우 증상을 설명할 때 필요한 표현들

1) I lost my glasses.

2) I have a fever.

3) I need to refill my prescription.

4) I feel dizzy.

5) Her face is swollen.

6) My husband got a bad sunburn.

7) I have been coughing all night.

8) My son feels better than he did yesterday.

9) My daughter has been vomiting for four hours.

10) I think I sprained my ankle.

11) My wife got a rash on her arm.

12) I injured myself skiing.

Quiz

다음 대화에서 빈 칸에 들어갈 올바른 단어나 구는?

Museum Worker : The museum closes at 7:00 pm.

1. You : And what time _____ tomorrow?

① does it open   ② it opens   ③ opening

Museum Worker : The museum opens at 9:00 am.

2. You : And _____ is the admission?

① what money   ② what cost   ③ how much

Museum Worker : The admission fee is $8... $5 if you're a student.

3. You : And are there any special exhibitions _____ (=happening) right now?

① off   ② on   ③ at

Museum Worker : Yes, there's a special exhibition of Edward Hopper's early paintings.

4. You : Is this _____ in the price of admission?

① a cost   ② included   ③ with

Doctor : What seems to be the problem?

5. You : I haven't been feeling well... I have been _____ (=vomiting) for the past 12 hours.

① throwing   ② discharging   ③ throwing up

Doctor : I see.... And do you have a fever?

6. You : Yes, I checked my _____ two hours ago. It was 101 (38.5 c.)

① tab   ② temperature   ③ payment

Doctor : Hmmm.... Sounds like you got food poisoning. Does your body feel sore?

7. You : Yes, my body does _____ a little.

① pain   ② cash   ③ hurt

Doctor : OK. I'm going to prescribe an antibiotic... Penicillin....

8. You : I'm _____ to Penicillin... Could you prescribe another one?

① allergic   ② sick   ③ reacting

Doctor : Oh, OK. I'll prescribe another one.... Take one pill every six hours, drink plenty of water, and stay in bed for the next 24 hours.

Sightseeing : Questions

1. Is this painting (by/from) Picasso?

2. Can you (take/make) a photo of me?

3. Are the restrooms in the (deep/back)?

4. Is this map (free/priceless)?

5. When does the next tour (start/starting)?

6. Is there a (sale/discount) for seniors?

7. Is there a tourist (knowledge/information) center around here?

8. Do you have any (bilingual/bi-language) brochures?

9. Is the museum (open/working) on Mondays?

10. Do you have an (ear/audio) guide?

 Vocabulary

1. sway = swing, move from side to side
2. pet = stroke, touch, petting zoo
3. prohibit = forbid, restrict
4. mention = state, say
5. sore = stinging, burning

Answers

1. does it open	2. how much	3. on
4. included	5. throwing up	6. temperature
7. hurt	8. allergic	

Sightseeing : Answers

1. from	2. take	3. back
4. free	5. start	6. discount
7. information	8. bilingual	9. open
10. audio		

Chapter 8 태국에서 여행자에게 필요한 영어(Tourist English in Thailand)

- 영화 '왕과 나(The King & I)' 관광

1. 대화(Target Language)

배낭을 메고 나 자신을 만나기 위해 떠나는 여행은 일상생활을 벗어남과 동시에 여행의 기쁨과 두려움으로 긴장의 연속이다. 여행지에서의 삶은 또 하나의 일상이므로 자는 것, 먹는 것 그 외 예상치 못한 일과의 만남들에 대한 상황을 머릿속에 최대한 많이 떠올려보는 것이 중요하다. 그러면 신속한 대처요령도 동시에 익힐 수 있게 된다. 여행자에게 필요한 많은 표현을 배워보자.

Tourist Questions

여행자에게 지도를 보고 길을 묻는 일은 하루의 일과 중 가장 중요한 부분이 될 것이다. 현지인도 가끔 엉뚱한 길을 가르쳐줄 수 있으니 가능한 반복해서 확인하는 것이 좋다.

가이드는 버스를 타고 이동할 경우 버스 기사와도 끊임없이 소통해야 한다.

"곧 저 다리를 지날 거죠?"라고 할 때
Are we going to pass the bridge?

곧 특이한 뭔가를 보게 될까요?
Are we going to see anything particular?

그것이 좌/우측에 있나요?
Is it on the right or the left?

안 보이는데… 다시 좀 손가락으로 콕 찍어주시겠습니까?
I don't see it. Can you point it out again?

내가 그것을 놓쳤나요?
Did I miss it?

우리가 돌아오는 길에 볼 수 있을까요?
Will we see it on the way back?

우리 지금 어디로 가고 있는 거죠?
Where are we headed (going) now?

여기서 더 이상 뭔가 할 일이 있을까요?
What else is there to do here?

당신은 어느 것을 권유하시렵니까?

Which do you recommend?

여기서 사진 찍어도 될까요?

Are we allowed to take pictures?

저~기, 저것은 무엇인가요?

What's that over there? (tourist points)

그것을 사려고 하는데 어디가 가장 좋을까요?

Where's the best place to buy that?

여기서 가장 가까운 화장실이 어딘지 아세요?

Do you know where the nearest washroom is?

가장 가까운 은행은?

Could you tell us where the nearest bank is?

혹시 구급약통 갖고 있나요?

You don't happen to have a first-aid kit, do you?

🎞 영화 '왕과 나'

젊은 미망인 안나(데보라 카)는 시암(Siam : 태국) 왕의 초청을 받고 아들 루이(렉스 톰슨)와 함께 방콕에 도착하지만 도착한 첫날부터 자신과의 약속을 지키지 않는 왕(율 브린너)에게 실망, 영국으로 돌아가려 한다. 정숙한 영국 여인 안나는 다소 거칠고 자기밖에 모르는 왕과 사사건건 충돌하지만 그러는 사이 시암의 근대화를 위해 다방면으

로 노력하는 왕에게 묘한 애정을 느낀다.

한편, 시암의 왕을 야만인이라고 모함하는 말이 영국 여왕의 귀에 들어가자 왕은 심각한 고민에 빠지고 이에 안나는 영국 대사에게 성대한 연회를 베풀어 왕이 야만인이 아니라는 걸 보여주자고 제안한다. 안나의 지도하에 만찬 주연은 잘 이루어지고, 연회의 하이라이트인 연극은 시암 왕에게 선물로 바쳐진 링버마의 공주 텁팀(리타 모레노)에 의해 성황리에 끝이 나 영국 대사 일행에게 깊은 감동을 안겨준다.

그러나 텁팀은 자신을 수행하고 온 사신, 룬타(카를로스 리바스)와 사랑하는 사이이며 그와 도망간 사실을 안 왕은 안나와 크게 언쟁을 하고 결국 안나는 영국으로 돌아갈 것을 결심하는데…

Asking for Directions

Could you tell me how to get to Grand Palace?

How do I find the taxi stand?

Pardon me, I'm lost, how do I get to the bookstore?

영화 속 대화 : The King and I - 1956

King : You will order the finest gold chopsticks.

Anna : Your Majesty, chopsticks?

King : I make mistake, the British not scientific enough to know how to use chopsticks.

2. 태국(Thailand) 소개

Suppose that you're anxious to explore Southeast Asia. Yet you don't want to get caught in the middle of a military junta suppressing the populace (Burma/ Myanmar). You don't want to run afoul of the law if you happen to play a song by a Jewish composer (Malaysia). You don't want to be killed by unexploded

ordnance (Vietnam). You don't want to be psychologically scarred by meeting people whose entire families were killed by the Khmer Rouge (Cambodia). You don't want to be out of reach of Western comforts (Laos). Where does that leave you?

In Thailand, the best country for beginners to Southeast Asia. Thailand has a per capita income of around $7000 per year, an extensive network of paved roads, a comprehensive mobile phone service, and quite a few world-class hotels, resorts, and restaurants.

Bangkok itself is a sprawling mess of a city, rather like Los Angeles : pollution, heat, and traffic (plus the added bonus of high humidity). For a photographer, however, it is notable as (1) the home of some important temples and palaces, and (2) the gateway to the rest of Thailand.

1) Old Royal City

Start where the rest of the tourists start : the Royal Grand Palace and associated temples. Be careful to leave your heavy artillery back in the hotel, however. Signs in several places prohibit the use of video cameras and still cameras with film larger than 35mm--if you wanted to see a Hasselblad with a red X through it, this is the place. Hauling out a tripod would definitely be a good way to attract the attention of the ubiquitous guards, many of whom carry automatic rifles.

Just south of the Grand Palace is Bangkok's oldest and largest temple complex : Wat Po. Most of the structures date from around 1800. The main temple (Bot) is billed by Carl Parkes as "among the most elegant in all of Thailand and a masterpiece of Thai religious architecture." Tough to photograph, though, given the close quarters. The 46-meter long 15-meter high gilded Reclining Buddha is not to be missed though. Security is a lot less heavy in Wat Po than at the Grand Palace.

After touring all the sights within the Wat Po complex you're probably tired. Stop at the massage school against the eastern wall and treat yourself to a one-hour session.

With a new spring in your massaged feet, walk two blocks north and then two blocks straight west from Wat Po to the river. Grab the city ferry (2 baht or about $0.05) across to river to Wat Arun. If you've still got the energy and it isn't a Monday or Tuesday, take the ferry back across and catch a taxi or tuk-tuk for a 5-minute ride to the National Museum.

2) Damnern Saduak Floating Market

If you liked The Man with the Golden Gun (1973), you'll love the floating market and long-tailed speed boats at the Damnern Saduak floating market, about a two-hour drive west from Bangkok. The authentic local-to-local action takes place starting at 0500. Busloads of tourists from Bangkok begin arriving at 0930 and disfigure the scene to a large extent.

If you're serious about photographing the life of the canals and the Thai-to-Thai floating market, you should probably stay overnight at Ban Sukchoke Resort (+66 32 253044, fax 254301) and catch a boat to the market in the first light.

3) Kanchanaburi

If you're on a bus tour, Kanchanaburi is where you stop to see the Bridge on the River Kwai, made famous in Pierre Boulle's novel and David Lean's movie (1957). If you're touring Thailand at a civilized pace, Kanchanaburi is where you'd stop for a week to take some boat rides, visit waterfalls in the local national parks, take a train ride on the railway whose construction killed 100,000 people.

The Allied War Cemetery is just a few minutes away from the bridge itself.

4) Nakhon Pathom

The first Buddhist settlement in Thailand was here in Nakhon Pathom, 54 km west of Bangkok, in the 6th century A.D. Any bus tour to the west of Bangkok will bring you back through this town to see the the world's largest chedi, 120 meters high and built starting in 1860.

5) Shopping

If you've got only a few hours in which to accomplish a lot of shopping, concentrate on the area near the World Trade Center mall, just east of Siam Square. The mall itself contains the Isetan Japanese department store. Across the street is Narayana Phand, the largest handicraft emporium in Thailand. Between the Regent Hotel and Grand Hyatt Erawan hotels is the Peninsula Plaza with high fashion boutiques and Asia Books, where you can find a lot of English titles.

If you've a special interest in antiques and reproductions, stop at the River City shopping center, which is indeed on the river and right next to the Sheraton Royal Orchid Hotel.

6) Restaurants

The good news for gourmets is that McDonald's is well-established in

Thailand. The bad news is that K C is even better established.

Even when you can't find a McDonald's, the quality of food is uniformly very high and prices are quite low. ood and water safety are quite good but Thais don't drink tap water. Bottled water is readily available and absurdly cheap. Given that a meal in the fanciest hotel costs only 10-20 per person, there isn't much reason to take a chance on a dirty restaurant.

7) Hotels

If you're young, poor, and in love with crowds and noise you'll want to stay in one of the famous backpacker guesthouses on Khao San Road, a short walk from the sights of the Old Royal City. To get a room, the guidebooks caution that you must arrive early in the day. The sidewalks are so packed with oversized foreigners shopping for trinkets that you'll literally be forced into the street if you want to get from one end of the block to another. If you're interested in peace, quiet, or authentic Thai culture, however, you'd do better to stay in absolutely any other part of the city.

If you're old and rich, most people would tell you to stay on the river in the Oriental Hotel where you can still see the ghosts of Somerset Maugham and Conrad. Take the advice if you don't mind the fact that the these ghosts today are mostly obscured by mobs of fat New orkers clamoring for help from the concierge. Locals aren't fond of the Oriental, claiming that the rooms are tiny and not worth the price.

If you want to avoid Bangkok's horrific traffic and get to and from tourist attractions via the river, stay at the Shangri-La, just a few blocks downriver from the Oriental. This is a much more spacious hotel than the Oriental and nearly all the common areas and restaurants enjoy views of the river.

Any hotel built around a koi pond is my kind of place and as an added bonus the Regent Bangkok (not the Indra Regent) is in most respects what you'd expect from the our Seasons chain. The one area where the Regent goes way beyond expectations is the 25-meter outdoor pool. An area where it falls short is Internet connectivity.

Their Web site advertises Internet connection in the rooms so you arrive expecting to plug an Ethernet cable into your network card and blast away at 1.5 Mbits. Instead what is delivered is 28.8K modem-based connectivity.

At 15 per hour The throughput actually delivered was closer to 2K bits per second and it took two or three hours to download a batch of email messages. If business requires you to work in the center of town, or if you love shopping malls, the Regent is a great choice at about 170 per night.

8) Guidebooks

or cultural background and a personal perspective, pick up Bangkok Handbook (Carl Parkes Moon). Dorling Kindersley Thailand contains a large Bangkok section and thumbnail photos of all the relevant sights.

No matter how many guidebooks you have, Bangkok will defy your attempts to orient yourself. The solution is to immediately buy a good map. Nelles Maps's Bangkok is excellent. Guidebooks will tell you to get Nancy Chandler's or Groovy Map and Guide of Bangkok .

9) Getting Around

Taxis in Bangkok are cheap, with a 20-minute ride seldom costing more than 2 or . nfortunately, the 20-minute ride might only take you four or five blocks in rush hour. ortunately, all taxis are air conditioned. nfortunately not all taxis have meters and negotiating with taxi drivers is annoying--wait for a cab with a Taximeter sign on the room. If you like the sensation of movement you may prefer to take the Skytrain, an elevated rail system, or river boats.

Electricity in Thailand is 220V at 50 Hz. Mechanically, the standard plug seems to be like the European two rounded prong plugs. Most laptop computer and digital camera power supplies can function on this power and at most you'll need a mechanical adaptor. Business hotel rooms often are equipped with an American-style plug near the desk.

The country code for Thailand is 66. If you're European or are an American GSM tri-band mobile phone owner, you'll find excellent GSM coverage throughout Thailand. Keep in mind that they use the European frequencies of 900 and 1800 MHz so an American Voicestream phone won't work unless you've had the foresight to get a special multi-frequency model.

Money is the baht. You can get cash with an American ATM card from just about any bank machine. The exchange rate was 44 baht per dollar in March 2001.

3. 상황별 대화(Conversation by Situation)

Sightseeing : Conversations while Sightseeing - 여행 안내소에서 대화

You : Hi, do you have any free maps of the city?

Tourist Information Center Worker : Yes, we do.... And we also have a free information booklet.

You : Great. Could we have one please?

Tourist Information Center Worker : Sure, here you go.

You : We're only here for one day. What do you recommend that we see?

Tourist Information Center Worker : Well, you can walk down Crescent Street. It has some beautiful historic architecture, and some good museums. Actually, that whole neighborhood is very interesting....

You : What's that neighborhood called?

Tourist Information Center Worker : Uptown.... When you go out, just turn right and in about three blocks you'll come to Crescent Street.

You : Great! We'll check it out. Oh, one more thing, could we use your bathroom?

Tourist Information Center Worker : Of course.

Meeting People 1 - 여행자와 여행자의 만남

Tom Sikorski : Hi, How are you?

You : Good, thanks. How are you? Are you also staying at this hotel?

Tom Sikorski : Yes, my wife and I are staying here. Where are you from?

You : I'm from Japan. What about you?

Tom Sikorski : I'm from Poland. How do you like Miami?

You : I like it very much. The weather is fantastic!

Tom Sikorski : Yes, it is. Are you traveling alone?

You : No, I'm here with my wife as well.

Tom Sikorski : Well, it was nice to meet you. My name is Tom, by the way....

You : Nice to meet you, Tom. I'm Hiro. Enjoy the rest of your stay!

Tom Sikorski : Thanks, Hiro. Take care!

Meeting People 2 - 길을 묻는 상황

Mary Rogers : Hi, can I help you find something?

You : Yes, I'm looking for the Guggenheim Museum... but I think I'm lost.

Mary Rogers : Oh! I'm going to the Guggenheim Museum. I'll show you where it is.

You : Thank you! I really appreciate that.

Mary Rogers : My name is Mary, by the way. Where are you from?

You : I'm from Italy. My name is Adriana.

Mary Rogers : Nice to meet you, Adriana. Are you studying here?

You : No, I'm just here on vacation.

Mary Rogers : And how do you like New York?

You : I like it very much. It's a very interesting place.

Talking to People : Making Small Talk - 여행자와 지역민의 대화

Alejandro : Excuse me, is the City Museum around here?

You : I don't know. I don't live here.

Alejandro : Oh! Where are you from?

You : I'm from South Africa.... I'm here on holiday.

Alejandro : I'm not from here either. I'm from Argentina. I'm studying at the university.

You : Oh, yeah? What are you studying?

Alejandro : Architecture.... What about you? Are you a student?

You : No, I graduated last year. I studied Nursing.

Alejandro : That's a really good profession. There's a lot of demand for it these days.

You : Yes, it's hard work, but I find it very rewarding. I like helping people.

Internet Cafes/Computers – 인터넷 카페에서의 대화

1) How much does it cost to use a computer for half an hour?

2) Do you have wireless internet access here?

3) I can't log on.

4) It's asking me for a password.

5) I need to check my e-mail.

6) Do you have headphones that I can use?

7) Can I get a coffee, please.

8) Do you serve food here?

9) I need to scan my passport.

10) Can I print something?

11) How much do I owe you?

12) I was on connected for 25 minutes.

Safety/Crime – 위협을 느꼈거나 범죄를 당했을 때 필요한 표현

1) I was robbed.

2) Someone stole my passport.

3) That man hit me.

4) We need an ambulance.

5) It's an emergency!

6) I'm going to call the police.

7) Leave me alone!

8) Help!

9) Officer, could you help me please?

10) Is it safe to walk at night in this neighborhood?

Quiz

다음 대화에서 빈 칸에 들어갈 올바른 단어나 구는?

1. You : Hi, do you have any free _____ of the city?

① carts   ② maps   ③ cards

Tourist Information Center Worker : Yes, we do.... And we also have a free information booklet.

2. You : Great. Could we _____ please?

① have one   ② make it   ③ give one

Tourist Information Center Worker : Sure, here you go.

3. You : We're only here for one day. What _____ that we see?

① you say   ② do you recommend   ③ do you want

Tourist Information Center Worker : Well, you can walk down Crescent Street. It has some beautiful historic architecture, and some good museums. Actually, that whole neighborhood is very interesting....

4. You : What's that neighborhood _____?

① called   ② said   ③ known

 Vocabulary

1. particular = special
2. headed = going
3. fever = temperature
4. sprain = twist
5. rash = pimple, eruption, 뾰루지
6. cold = influenza, flu
7. cough = 기침
8. ache = ill, hurt, sick, headache, earache, backache, stomachache

Answers

1. maps	2. have one
3. do you recommend	4. called

스페인에서 전화하기
(On the Telephone in Spain)

Chapter **9**

- 영화 '내 남자의 아내도 좋아(Vicky Christina Barcelona)' 관광

1. 대화(Target Language)

외국을 여행할 때 전화로 외국인에게 문의하는 것은 상당히 부담스러운 일이다. 얼굴을 보고 대화할 때에는 제스처를 사용하거나 표정으로 의사소통을 할 수 있으나 단지 목소리만을 사용하여 상대방에게 내가 원하는 것을 이해시킨다는 것은 쉬운 일이 아니다. 특히 전화상으로 고객의 메시지를 받고 전달하는 일은 평소 훈련되어 있어 있지 않으면 자칫 고객에게 실수를 할 수 있다. 그러므로 평소에 적절한 전화표현과 전화 매너를 익혀두도록 하자.

전화받을 때
Hello
May I help you?
OOO speaking!

전화했는데 다른 사람이 전화를 받았을 때 OOO씨를 바꿔달라고 해야겠지요?
Is Mr. _____ there (in)?
May I speak to Ms. _____?
I would like to speak to Mr. _____.

수화기를 들고 "잠깐만 기다리세요"라고 하고 싶으면

Hold on, please.

내가 받은 전화를 다른 객실이나 사무실로 돌려줄 때

I'll transfer you to _____.

I'll put you through.

"제가 전화 다시 드리겠습니다"라고 하고 싶으면

I'll call back.

I'm returning your call.

고객에게 "메시지를 남기시겠느냐"고 물어볼 때

Could you leave a message for her/him?

I got your message.

Role Play Activity for Telephone Use(전화로 메시지를 받는 역할극)

Message 1 - A is Calling, B is Taking Message

고객이 메시지를 전해 달라고 할 때는 정해진 양식에 따라 상세히 남기되 누가 누구에게 전달하는 것인지, 내용은 무엇인지를 적고 전화받은 시간과 통화자 본인의 이름을 상세히 기록해 둔다.

Information for A and information for B

Name of caller : William Keller Johanson can't answer : Out of office

Name of person wanted : Samuel Miller

Reason for call : Meeting canceled

Message : Reschedule for Wednesday at 10:30

Message Memo

Date   : _____

Time : _____

To : _____

Message : _____

_____

_____

Message 2 - A is Calling, B is Taking a Message

Information for A and Information for B

Name of caller : Lydia Lynn Johanson can't answer : On another line

Name of person wanted : Matthew Brian Goer

Reason for call : Thompson merger

Message : Call office ASAP

Message Memo

Date : _____

Time : _____

To : _____

Message : _____

_____

_____

⊛ 영화 '내 남자의 아내도 좋아(Vicky Christina Barcelona)' 관광

바르셀로나로 휴가를 떠난 두 친구 앞에 전개되는 전혀 예상할 수 없었던 사랑이야 기를 다룬 '내 남자의 아내도 좋아'. 이 영화의 원제는 Vicky Christina Barcelona이다. 이 영화는 바르셀로나를 배경으로 하는데 아름답고 경이로운 바르셀로나 곳곳을 보여 주고 있다. 구엘공원, 카사밀라 등 가우디의 건축물도 미리 만나볼 수 있다. 로맨스라

면 고통도 달콤하다고 느낄 정도로 사랑 앞에 용감한 크리스티나(스칼렛 요한슨)와 로맨틱한 낭만보다는 이성이 앞서는 지적인 현실주의자 비키(레베카 홀). 가장 친한 친구지만, 사랑에 관해서는 완전히 상반된 생각을 가지고 있는 두 사람은 바르셀로나로 휴가를 떠난다. 달콤한 지중해의 바르셀로나에서 휴가를 즐기던 두 사람은 우연히 매력적인 화가 후안 안토니오(하비에르 바르뎀)를 만나게 되고, 그의 노골적인 유혹에 강하게 거부하는 비키와 달리 크리스티나는 후안에게 묘한 매력을 느낀다.

하지만 얘기치 않은 순간에 비키마저 후안에게 빠져들지만, 예정된 결혼을 위해 바르셀로나를 떠난다. 그리고 바르셀로나에 남게 된 크리스티나와 후안이 둘만의 사랑을 나누던 어느 날, 후안의 전처 마리아(페넬로페 크루즈)가 둘 사이에 나타난다. 그들의 불안정한 동거생활도 잠시, 어느새 가까워진 마리아와 크리스티나는 사랑을 나누게 되는데…

Asking for Directions

Could you tell me how to get to Barcelona?

How do I find the Sagrada Familia by Gaudi?

Pardon me, I'm lost, how do I get to the La Rambla?

영화 속 대화

Maria Elena : You speak no Spanish?

Cristina : No, uh-uh studied Chinese.

Maria Elena : Chinese? Why?

Cristina : I thought it sounded pretty.

Maria Elena : Say something in Chinese.

Cristina : Me?

Maria Elena : Mm-hm.

Cristina : Um... ni hao ma?

Maria Elena : You think that sounds pretty?

2. 바르셀로나(Barcelona) 소개

Barcelona is a medieval city surrounded by baroque quarters surrounded by the finest Modernista buildings (Spanish Art Nouveau, notably the architecture of Antoni Gaudi). For the 1992 Olympic Games the city was blessed with a wealth of modern recreational facilities.

With its sunny Mediterranean climate and winter temperatures in the 50s and 60s, Barcelona can be enjoyed as a weekend escape from gloom and grey. The city is also a good base for exploring the small towns and wild coast of Catalonia.

1) Safety

Here's an excerpt from a 4-star hotel's information guide : "Supervise and control your luggage : Do not leave it unattended even for a minute. Be extremely careful with your baggage while paying for your stay." I would have laughed if I'd not recalled that my parents had their carry-on bag stolen, right from the lobby, while checking into a $150/night hotel near La Rambla. Their experience is reflected in the architecture of the Hotel Arts, built for the 1992 Olympics.

From the street, the skyscraper looks like a fortress. There is a moat and no visible lobby. If you drive into the interior of the fortress you find a small elevator area and some bellmen. Take the elevator up one floor and you'll find yourself in the lobby.

The officially published city guide cautions people with "handbags, cameras, video cameras, etc." The same guide warns you especially against people offering flowers on the street getting close to you or someone saying that you have a stain on your clothing.

The Old Town, away from La Rambla, is particularly dangerous at night. A lot of restaurants and cafes try to make sure that their patrons still have enough to pay the bill at the end of the night by hiring private security guards to stand out front.

The Dorling Kindersley guide advises keeping cards and money in a belt. The official guide advises leaving your passport with the hotel and carrying a photocopy. If you're concentrating on photography, your chances of being a victim rise to nearly 100 percent. If it is cold enough for a jacket, choose one with a zippered interior pocket and use that for cards and most of your cash. If the weather is hot, get a money belt.

Women should not carry anything valuable in a purse. Unless you have an assistant whose only job is to safeguard a camera bag, don't carry extra lenses. One camera. One lens. In your hands at all times.

2) Modernista Architecture and Antoni Gaudi

Barcelona offers many of the charms of other European cities, including a cathedral, Baroque palaces, and a smattering of modern successes. Uniquely, though, Barcelona displays the work of imaginative architects working from 1885 through around 1910. This was the Catalonian response to the Art Nouveau movement and the best-known architect is Antoni Gaudi (1852-1926). In one day you can see most of the important Gaudi buildings.

Start at the Sagrada Familia, the church that Gaudi started in 1883 and that still isn't done. In the summer, get there at

9:00 am sharp to avoid long lines. If you are stuck on the line at the ticket booth, be wary of women trying to pin flowers on your clothing. Once inside, you have the opportunity to take an elevator or walk to the top of one of the towers on the east side of the church.

The museum in the basement of the church is worthwhile. It includes a model used by Gaudi to determine the structure that would support itself using the minimum material.

Hop a cab to the Parc Guell, in the northeast corner of downtown. Remember to watch your camera, wallet, etc., inside the park!

Walk three blocks south from Casa Mila to the Illa de la Discordia (Island of Discord), a single block along the Passeig de Gracia containing four Modernista buildings by different architects. The most interesting is Gaudi's Casa Batllo.

3) The Beach Scene

To photograph people enjoying the beach, start in Barceloneta, a complex of narrow streets and houses built for the working class. The district is surrounded by a yacht harbor on one side and a sandy beach on the other. There is a covered market in the main square.

Barcelonans predict rapid gentrification of this district but in the meantime you can get some photos of old neighbors hanging out laundry and chatting. Unless it is raining, skip the Museum of the History of Catalonia (photography prohibited; most signs only in Spanish and Catalan).

4) The Old City

The oldest part of the city is the area around the cathedral, built starting in 1298. The streets are narrow and open into small squares.

Skip the Picasso Museum but do go into the Museu d'Art Contemporani, a 1995 success by Richard Meier, architect of California's New Getty, just off La Rambla. The building is much nicer than the art; photography permitted without flash or tripod.

Note that, according to the concierge at my hotel, the old city is not safe at night.

5) Montjuic

Take a taxi to the Fundacion Joan Miro, up on the hill in Montjuic. Photography is permitted without flash or tripod.

A five-minute walk will take you to the Olympic stadium and its unusual radio tower. From there a rather tiring 20-minute walk, with occasional views out to the sea, will take you to Poble Espanyol (Spanish Village). This is a strange collection of 116 reproduction buildings from different cities in Spain.

6) Parc de la Ciutadella

Parc de la Ciutadella, just to the east of the Old City, contains a small zoo, several museums and important Modernista fountains and sculpture.

7) La Rambla

One of the most famous streets in Spain, La Rambla runs through the Old City right down to the harbor. The wide center strip is devoted to newsstands, flower merchants, performers, and hordes of pedestrians. On either side of this strip are busy lanes for cars and buses. Next to the car/bus lanes are shops, restaurants, hotels, and the twice-burned opera house.

8) Photographic Exhibitions

Pick up a copy of Guia del Ocio (www.guiadelociobcn.es) at a newsstand for full listings of photography shows at galleries and museums.

9) Just for Fun

The one absolute must for nightlife in Barcelona is a concert at the Palau de la Musica Catalana, a Modernista triumph in the Old City. Stop by the hall during the daytime to buy tickets at the box office and also to by tickets for a guided tour in English during the day. The acoustics of the hall are superb and any group booked into the Palau is going to be good. It is small hall by modern standards so don't worry too much about where you sit. The 1980s renovation included the installation of air conditioning.

It really isn't much of a photographic subject, but L'Aquarium shouldn't be missed. It is the largest aquarium in Europe and includes two long underwater tunnels. The aquarium is open until 9:00 pm and is on the harbor, behind the Maremagnum shopping center, directly across a footbridge from La Rambla. Flash photography is prohibited. If you're determined to take some photos, be prepared with a fast lens and ISO 800 or ISO 1600 film.

10) Shops and Photo Labs

For standard professional camera gear, visit ARPI on La Rambla. Since they carry Hasselblad, Linhof, and Rollei they can presumably direct you to the best labs in town. For one-stop shopping, including a traditional souvenir selection, try the huge department store El Corte Ingles ("The English Cut", referring to its origins selling men's suits) on Placa Catalunya (north tip of La Rambla).

For buying food and taking photos of people buying food, La Boqueria on La Rambla is unparalleled.

For an Internet fix, visit the 24-hour easy.

Everything cafe on La Rambla.

11) Hotels

If you need Internet connectivity from your room, you're out of luck! As far as I can tell, there aren't any hotels in Barcelona with 10base-T jacks in the rooms.

Most people would tell you to stay on or just off La Rambla. If you want to step out of your hotel into a crowd, a hooker (after 10:00 pm), a pickpocket (anytime), etc., this is good advice. If the crowds of La Rambla, especially in the summertime, put you off, consider going south to the port or north into the Eixample neighborhood. Remember that Spain is a country of mopeds; any hotel room overlooking a street will be noisy.

If you want to wake up and look at the ocean every morning, Hotel Arts is for you (+34 93 221 1000; fax 221 1070). There are 500 rooms packed into one of the tallest buildings in Spain, smack on the Port Olimpic yacht harbor. Minuses : you'll be taking a taxi or the subway to the center of town; once you're in the hotel, you might as well be in Las Vegas.

12) Restaurants

The Michelin Red Guides are the most reliable source for restaurants throughout Europe. If you care about food, you'll definitely want the Michelin Red Guide Spain and Portugal. To an American palette, Catalan cuisine seems to be based on salt, seafood, and pork. If you like paella, you'll be happy here. If you yearn for broccoli, you might have to buy it yourself at La Boqueria, the covered market off La Rambla.

Established in 1870, Restaurant Puda Can Manel is one of the best places in town for seafood. It is in Barceloneta at Passeig Joan de Borbo, 60. This street borders the harborfront. Call 93 221 50 13 to reserve a table. The outdoor tables are ideally positioned to catch afternoon sunshine.

All of the fast food chains are here. Fresh and Ready is a sandwich and salad chain with an English menu and a reasonable selection of vegetarian food. It is the Barcelonan equivalent of London's Pret a Manger.

13) Guidebooks

Dorling Kindersley's Barcelona and Catalonia is below the standard of the publisher's other guidebooks, but still useful for a photographer because of the small snapshots of each site. Thus you're able to make an informed decision as to whether or not the journey will be photographically worthwhile.

For details on art and architecture, get the Blue Guide to Barcelona. TimeOut

Barcelona should have the most up-to-date nightlife and beach scene discussion. You'd think that Lonely Planet would be good for people on a low budget but the Amazon reader reviews indicate otherwise (and also warn about being "violently mugged less than a block from my hotel off of La Rambla").

14) Getting There

You can get a non-stop flight into Barcelona from most European capitals. A taxi from the airport to downtown is about $15.

For airline choices, see the photo.net guide to international airlines. You may wish to avoid Virgin Express, the horror of which cannot be overstated.

15) Getting Around

Taxis in Barcelona are inexpensive but you've got about a 1 in 10 chance of a driver taking you around in circles. Unless you're an absolutely fluent Spanish speaker, point to your desired destination on a map. The subway and bus system is comprehensive.

3. 상황별 대화(Conversation by Situation)

At the Hotel 1 : At the VIP Lounge - 호텔에서 야외활동을 위해 문의

Staff : VIP Lounge. How can I help you?

Guest : Yes, this is Mrs. Turner in room 2110. I'd like to arrange an elephant ride for my daughter.

Staff : Certainly ma'am. When would you like to go?

Guest : How about 10:00 am?

Staff : Would you also like me to arrange transportation to and from the ride?

Guest : That would be great, if it's not too much trouble.

Staff : No trouble at all ma'am. If you could meet me in the VIP Lounge at 10:00 I'll escort you to the taxi.

Guest : Sounds great. I'll see you then.

Staff : See you at 10:00 Goodbye.

At the Hotel 2 : Ordering to Room Service - 객실에서 룸서비스로 음식을 주문하는 상황

Staff : Room Service, how can I help you?

Guest : Yes, could you send up a BLT, a bag of chips, and an ice tea.

Staff : Of course Sir, could I have your room number?

Guest : It's 1515.

Staff : OK, your order will be there in about 15 minutes.

Guest : Thank you, goodbye.

At the Hotel 3 : Calling to Housekeeping - 객실에서 담요를 추가 요청

Staff : Housekeeping, how can I be of assistance?

Guest : Could I have a couple more blankets sent up to my room please.

Staff : Of course ma'am. Could I have your room number.

Guest : I'm in room 777.

Staff : They will be there in 10 minutes.

Guest : Thanks. Bye.

Staff : You're welcome, have a good night.

At the Hotel 4 : Taking a Message - 전화로 메시지를 받는 상황

Caller : May I speak to Mr. Morrison please?

Staff : He is not in at the moment. Can I take a message?

Caller : Yes, could you tell him that Julie Anderson called.

Staff : Could I have your number please?

Caller : Yes, it's 555-6709.

Staff : I'll give him the message.

Caller : Thanks, bye.

At the Hotel 5 : Delivering a Message - 전화로 메시지를 전달하는 상황

Staff : Is this the Gillett room?

Guest : Yes, it is.

Staff : May I speak to Mr. Gillett?

Guest : He's not here, he's at the pool. Shall I have him call you back?

Staff : Yes please, have him call the front desk. It's about the change in his departure flight.

Guest : I'll give him the message.

Staff : Thanks, bye.

At the Hotel 6 : Getting from the Hotel into the City - 객실에서 프런트 클럭에게 전화를 걸어 호텔 앞으로 택시를 불러달라는 상황

You : How do I get to downtown from here? Can I take a bus or do I have to take a taxi?

Hotel Clerk : There are no buses that go to downtown from here. You'll have to take a cab.

You : And how much does that cost?

Hotel Clerk : The fare to downtown is usually about $20. Would you like me to call you one?

You : Sure, can I get one for 2:00 pm?

Hotel Clerk : Absolutely. It'll be waiting for you in front of the hotel. Is there anything else I can do for you?

You : Yes, can you get someone to change the sheets in my room?

Hotel Clerk : Yes, of course.

You : Thanks. You've been very helpful.

At the Hotel 7 : Making a Reservation - 객실을 예약하는 상황

Hotel Clerk : The Four Seasons Hotel. How can I help you?

You : Hello, My name is Mr. Wong. I'd like to reserve a room. Do you have any available from March 10th to March 13th?

Hotel Clerk : Yes, we do. Would you like a double room or a single room?

You : How much is the double room per night?

Hotel Clerk : It's $75 per night.... And the single room is $65 per night.

You : I'm looking for a room that would be nice for a romantic weekend. Which of the two do you recommend?

Hotel Clerk : I'd go with the smaller one, the single room. It's much nicer.... And two people can stay in that room.

You : OK, perfect. I'd like to reserve that one then.

Hotel Clerk : Alright. I've made that reservation for you. And how will you be arriving?

You : We'll be arriving by car.

Hotel Clerk : Perfect. We have an underground lot where you can park your car.

Quiz

다음 대화에서 빈 칸에 들어갈 올바른 단어나 구는?

Hotel Clerk : The Four Seasons Hotel. How can I help you?

1. You : Hello, My name is Mr. Wong. I'd like to reserve a room. Do you have
_____ from March 10th to March 13th?

① any available   ② free   ③ some free

Hotel Clerk : Yes, we do. Would you like a double room or a single room?

2. You : _____ the double room per night?

① What costs   ② How much is   ③ What is the price

Hotel Clerk : It's $75 per night.... And the single room is $65 per night.

3. You : And how much does that _____?

① expensive   ② spent   ③ cost

Hotel Clerk : The fare to downtown is usually about $20. Would you like me
to call you one?

You : Sure, can I get one for 2:00 pm?

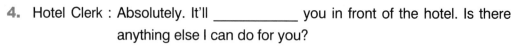

4. Hotel Clerk : Absolutely. It'll _____ you in front of the hotel. Is there anything else I can do for you?

① wait for   ② come to   ③ be waiting for

 Vocabulary

1. BLT = Bacon, Lettuce, Tomato
2. cab = taxi
3. fare = charge, fee
4. excerpt = extract, selection, chosen one

Answers

1. any available   2. How much is
3. cost   4. be waiting for

스위스에서 표 구매하기
(Ticketing in Switzerland)

Chapter **10**

- 알프스의 '하이디(Heidi, Girl of the Alps)' 관광

1. 대화(Target Language)

여행 중 교통비용(transportation expense)을 절약하기 위해서는 가능한 한 사전예약을 하는 것이 중요하다. 스위스 열차예약은 www.sbb.ch 창에서 간단하게 예약할 수 있으며 때론 반값 티켓 구매도 가능하다. 또한 편도(single)보다는 왕복(return) 티켓을 구매하는 경우 기간에 따라 30~50%까지 교통비를 아낄 수 있으니 여행 목적지에 관한 철저한 사전 준비를 해보자. 유럽의 지붕 융프라우에 가거나 소설의 주인공 하이디의 배경지인 마이엔펠트를 찾아가는 길에 이용하는 교통편을 위한 티케팅에 필요한 표현을 익혀보자.

Timetable & ticket sales

From:	Station, city, point of interest
To:	Station, city, point of interest
Via:	Station, city, point of interest

Tu, 09.08.16   ◀ ▶   ▦   03:32

Dep **Arr**   **Search connection**

➤ **Advanced search**

ℹ **Rail traffic information**

A : Hello.

B : Hi. What time is the next flight to Luzern?

A : At 3:00 this afternoon.

B : I'd like to buy a ticket.

A : Ok. What's your name?

B : Lookey Hansen.

A : Can you spell that?

B : Sure. Lookey is L-O-O-K-E-Y and Hansen is spelled H-A-N-S-E-N.

A : And your address?

B : 3462 First Avenue Luzern 33056.

A : What's your phone number?

B : Area code (305) 452-2459.

A : Ok. Would you like a window or aisle seat?

B : Window, please.

A : How would you like to pay for your ticket?

B : With my credit card.

A : Ok. Here's your ticket.

☸ Heidi, Girl of the Alps in Switzerland

스위스 한 산골마을에 마을사람들과 잘 어울리지도 않고 냉담하며 비사교적이던 할아버지에게 도시에서 아들이 찾아오고 할아버지의 손녀인 하이디를 맡기고는 떠나버린다. 그렇게 하이디는 할아버지와 단둘이서 살게 되는데 처음에 할아버지에게 하이디는 귀찮고 불편한 존재였지만 시간이 흐르자 정이 드는데 어느 날 하이디의 고모인 다디의 강요로 어느 큰 도시 부잣집에 맡겨져 그 집 딸인 클라라의 친구로 지내게 된다. 그러나 시골이 그리운 하이디는 밤마다 외로워 울음을 터뜨리고 몽유병 환자가 되어 하얀 이불을 뒤집어쓰고 다닌다. 그 덕분에 집에 귀신소동이 일어나고 하이디가 시골을 그리워하는 것을 알게 된 클라라 아빠는 하이디를 스위스의 시골마을로 돌려보낸다. 그 후

하이디가 들려주던 시골마을을 보고 싶어하는 클라라의 요청으로 클라라의 가족은 하이디가 있는 산골마을에 오게 되고 덕분에 외롭게 살던 할아버지는 마음을 열고 마을 사람들과 어울리게 된다. 클라라 또한 시골에 와서 하이디와 양치기 소년 피터 등 산골마을 아이들과 어울려 놀다 보니 일어서서 걸을 수 있을 정도로 건강해진다.

Asking for Directions

Can you give me directions to Interlaken to go to Jungfraujoch

What's the best way to get to Maienfeld train station

It's on your right, next to the sign, Heidiwig.   ou can't miss it

소설 속 대사

The girl thus addressed stood still, and the child immediately let go her hand and seated herself on the ground.

"Are you tired, Heidi " asked her companion.

"No, I am hot," answered the child.

"We shall soon get to the top now.   ou must walk bravely on a little longer, and take good long steps, and in another hour we shall be there," said Dete in an encouraging voice.

They were now joined by a stout, good-natured-looking woman, who walked on ahead with her old acquaintance, the two breaking forth at once into lively conversation about everybody and everything in Dorfli and its surroundings, while the child wandered behind them.

"And where are you off to with the child?" asked the one who had just joined the party. "I suppose it is the child your sister left?"

"Yes," answered Dete. "I am taking her up to Uncle, where she must stay."

2. 스위스(Switzerland) 소개

Due to its small size in the center of Europe, the main attractions of Switzerland are concentrated within short distances of each other. Attractions and activities abound and traveling by train in Switzerland offers absolute freedom and flexibility. Wake up, have breakfast and then take a quick train ride to another city for lunch or shopping and be back in time for dinner!

The center stage of Switzerland is occupied by the Alps. They extend from the east of France to the west of Germany/Austria and are bordered by Italy in the south. North of the Alps a lowland area called the "Mittelland", hosts many beautiful lakes and most of the major cities before a smaller mountain range, the Jura, sets the division to the city of Basel and the river Rhein.

The Matterhorn in Zermatt is certainly the most famous of all mountain peaks and is a must for every visitor of Switzerland. Upon spotting the Matterhorn, which is part of the loftiest Alps in the Valais, you will be overwhelmingly excited by its impressive beauty. Experience the breathtaking scenery in this charming, traffic-free mountain resort.

The Bernese Oberland invites you with a great variety of attractions. An appealing countryside is speckled by enchanting lakes and flanked by impressive mountains, most importantly the Jungfraujoch, near Interlaken. Other Alpine and mountain resorts in the area include Gstaad, Grindelwald, Wengen and Muerren.

The fame of Lucerne as a tourist resort is legendary and it is often considered to be the true "Swiss" capital. This charming and attractive town straddles the Reuss River on the western edge of Lake Lucerne and makes an excellent base for excursions with its proximity to lakes and mountains as well as a base for venturing south towards the Alps and the Ticino. A good way to see Lucerne and Central Switzerland is from the Pilatus : a towering monument of a mountain with a view like a vision. It only takes one hour to reach the famous 7000-ft. landmark of Lucerne.

Switzerland's southernmost canton, Italian-speaking Ticino, can seem a world apart from the rest of the country, especially the lakeside resorts of Lugano and Locarno, with their Mediterranean Riviera like atmosphere. The romance that surrounds the southern part of Switzerland is well worth the visit.

Zurich, the most populous city of Switzerland, is famous for its financial institutions and shops on "Bahnhofstrasse" as well as for its superb art galleries - all coexisting happily side by side. Lake Zurich offers endless opportunities for swimming, sunbathing and pick nicking.

In the west, the cities lining the northern shore of Lake Geneva - Geneva, Montreux and Lausanne - are surrounded by rolling hills covered with woods and vineyards which shelter them from the north and east winds. This area makes up the bulk of French-speaking Switzerland.

Geneva is unquestionably one of Switzerland's most privileged cities on account of its exceptional location. Visitors will be delighted by opulent mansions, the harbor and its fountain, and the shimmering shores of the lake, set against a backdrop of lush vegetation and wooded mountains.

1) 유럽의 지붕이라 불리는 융프라우

The Jungfraujoch – Top of Europe is the most profitable segment of the Group. The core of this business is the highest railway station in Europe at 3,454 metres above sea level, situated within the UNESCO World Heritage Site SWISS ALPS Jungfrau-Aletsch.

The trip with the Wengernalp Railway and the Jungfrau Railway to the Jungfraujoch is also the strategic "heart" of the company. The previous attendance record was achieved in 2014 with 866,000 guests. This was equalled in 2015. Earlier than expected, with 1,007,000 visitors at the Top of Europe, the magical milestone of one million was reached.

The railway journey to the Jungfraujoch is an experience which leads through the Eiger and the Mönch. At the Eismeer and Eigerwand intermediate stations, visitors can enjoy the wonderful view.

The Jungfrau Railway Group is a leading tourism company and the largest mountain railway company in Switzerland. It offers its customers an adventure in the mountains and on the train. The main offer is the journey to the Jungfraujoch – Top of Europe. Due to the long-term development of a distribution and agency network, it has achieved a leading position in the Asian markets.

2) 하이디의 마을이라 불리는 스위스 마이엔펠트(Maienfeld) 기차역

Adelheid (called Heidi) is five years old when her aunt Dette, who has raised Heidi since her parents' death four years earlier, takes Heidi to live with her formidable grandfather on the Swiss Alps. Dette has found a promising job in

Frankfurt, but cannot leave while still Heidi's guardian.

The only relative left is Heidi's grandfather, and in Dette's opinion, he should take some responsibility. Alm-Onji (Alps-Uncle), as Heidi's grandfather is commonly known, has a fearsome reputation with the villagers of Dörfli, as rumors claim that in his youth he killed a man. Now he lives a solitary life with his dog Josef in a cabin halfway up the mountain.

However, Heidi quickly wins her way into his heart with her enthusiasm and intelligence, firmly establishing herself in his life. She spends her summer days on the mountain top with the goatherd Peter, whose responsibility it is to take the villagers' goats to the high mountains for pasture, and her winters occasionally visiting Peter's grandmother, a blind old woman whose dream is to one day hear her cherished book of psalms read to her. Alm-Onji's misanthropy prevents Heidi from going to school, of which she has no experience anyway.

Heidi continues to live happily in the mountains until Aunt Dette returns from the city, excited about a good opportunity for Heidi. A wealthy German business-man, Mr. Sesemann, is searching for a companion for his crippled daughter. distorted by Alm-Onji, Dette tricks Heidi into accompanying her, ostensibly to get a present for Peter and her grandfather. Promised that she can return at any time, Heidi is taken to Frankfurt.

There, Dette abandons her to the care of Miss Rottenmeier, the strict, no-nonsense governess in charge of Clara's welfare. Heidi and Clara quickly become friends, and Heidi quickly turns the household topsy-turvy with her escapades and well-meaning faux pas. Clara is enchanted by Heidi's stories of the Alps, which paint a picture of a life completely different from the sheltered and lonely one she is accustomed to. Her father is mostly away on business, and Clara's only constant companions until now are the servants and her canary.

Heidi's longing to return home and occasional attempts to escape are punctuated by the occasional distractions of new friends. She smuggles a small kitten into the house, and Clara and she care for it until Mrs. Rottenmeier discovers it and has it thrown out. Clara's doctor befriends her, and occasionally keeps a benevolent eye on her, but it is Clara's grandmother that has the most impact. On one of her rare visits to Frankfurt, she and Heidi become fast friends.

3. 상황별 대화(Conversation by Situation)

Ticketing : At the Railway Station - 융프라우에 가기 위해 인터라켄행 기차티케팅

Paul Ryefield	:	What time does the next train to Interlaken leave?
Railway Station Clerk	:	At 9:30, from platform 8.
Paul Ryefield	:	Is it a direct train to Interlaken?
Railway Station Clerk	:	No, you have to change trains at Lausanne?
Paul Ryefield	:	I see. 8 tickets to Interlaken, please.
Railway Station Clerk	:	Single or return, Sir?
Paul Ryefield	:	single, please.
Railway Station Clerk	:	550 CHF, please.
Paul Ryefield	:	Here you are.
Railway Station Clerk	:	Here's your ticket and change.

Buying Tickets 1 - 등급별 가격을 비교하면서 티케팅하는 상황

You : Hello. I would like two tickets to Zurich, please, for the 5:00 pm train if possible.

Clerk : First or second-class?

You : What's the difference in price between the two?

Clerk : First class tickets are 70 CHF each and second-class tickets are 35 CHE each.

You : Do you have anything cheaper?

Clerk : No, sorry, Sir. That's the lowest price I can get you for today or tomorrow.

You : I'll take two second-class tickets. Can I buy the return tickets now as well?

Clerk : If you like... When would you like to come back?

You : Is there a train that goes to Zurich in the afternoon on Monday?

Clerk : Yes... there's a train from Zurich to Luzern leaving daily at 4:00 pm... Would you like me to book two tickets for you?

You : Yes, please do. Second-class as well.

Buying Tickets 2 - 특별 D/C가 있을 경우 보통 현금지불을 요구하는 상황

You : Hello. Could I get two tickets to Geneva, please, for the 5:00 pm bus.

Clerk : Sure. That'll be 100 CHF.

You : Oh, I thought these tickets were on sale?

Clerk : They are, but only when you book two weeks in advance.

You : OK, no problem.... I'll take them. How much did you say they were?

Clerk : 100 CHF. You did want one-way tickets, not round-trip, right?

You : That's right. Can I pay by credit card?

Clerk : No, I'm sorry, we only accept cash.

You : OK, could you tell me where the nearest ATM(=cash machine) is?

Clerk : There's one in the bank across the street from here.

Quiz

다음 대화에서 빈 칸에 들어갈 올바른 단어나 구는?

1. You : I need a ticket to Miami, please, for today _____.

① perhaps   ② if possible   ③ can be

Ticket Counter Worker : All right.... Yes, I can get you on the flight at 7:00 pm tonight, which arrives in Miami at 10:00 pm. This ticket is $650.

2. You : Do you have anything _____?

① less   ② cheaper   ③ so expensive

Ticket Counter Worker : No, not on such short notice, Sir. That's the lowest price I can get you for today or tomorrow.

3. You : Hello. I _____ two tickets to Manchester, please, for the 5:00 pm train.

① would buy   ② would like   ③ would sell

Clerk : First or second-class?

4. You : What's the _____ between the two?

① difference in price   ② different price   ③ cheaper

Clerk : First class tickets are £47 each and second-class tickets are £35 each.

5. You : I'll take two second-class tickets. Can I buy the _____ tickets now as well?

① round　　② return　　③ back

Buying Tickets : Questions

1. Answer : It's the standard charge for the seat reservation.

Question : Why did you charge me €5 more?

Did you give me back my change?

Do I have to change trains?

2. Answer : No, only regular seats.

Question : How much is the ticket?

Does this train have sleeper seats?

Do I have to change trains?

3. Answer : Yes, it's 10% cheaper if you have your International Student Card.

Question : Can I get a student discount?

Is there a discount for seniors?

Is there another train to London today?

4. Answer : No, it's a direct train.

Question : Does this train have sleeper seats?

How much is the ticket?

Do I have to change trains?

5. Answer : No, we'll put them in the bus' baggage compartment.

Question : Did you find my bag?

Do I have to bring my bags on the bus?

Is this the only bus station in this city?

6. Answer : Yes, there are three stops before that station.

Question : Is this the only bus station in this city?

Are there any buses going to Charleston today?

Does the bus stop anywhere before the central bus station?

7. Answer : Yes, if it's not expired, you'll get back 70% of the ticket price.

Question : Can I get a refund (=money back) for an unused ticket?

Can I get a discount if I buy my ticket in advance?

Do you have a schedule I could look at?

8. Answer : If you buy your ticket one week in advance, it'll be 20% cheaper.

Question : Can I get a discount if I buy my ticket in advance?

Can I get a refund (=money back) for an unused ticket?

Do you have a schedule I could look at?

9. Answer : Yes, there's one at 10:00 am, and another at 5:45 pm.

Question : Can I get off before the central bus station?

Are there any buses going to Charleston today?

Is this the only bus station in town?

10. Answer : No, they leave from Victoria Station.

Question : How much is a ticket to Brussels?

How long is the trip to Brussels?

Do trains to Brussels leave from this station?

Vocabulary

1. window seat = seat next to window
2. aisle seat = seat next to corridor or walkway
3. book = reserve
4. formidable = intimidating, 겁나는
5. misanthropy = hate people
6. companion = friend
7. ostensibly = 표면상, 겉으로

Answers

1. if possible
2. cheaper
3. would like
4. difference in price
5. return

Buying Tickets : Answers

1. Why did you charge me €5 more?
2. Does this train have sleeper seats?
3. Can I get a student discount?
4. Do I have to change trains?
5. Do I have to bring my bags on the bus?
6. Does the bus stop anywhere before the central bus station?

7. Can I get a refund(= money back) for an unused ticket?

8. Can I get a discount if I buy my ticket in advance?

9. Are there any buses going to Charleston today?

10. Do trains to Brussels leave from this station?

터키에서 비행기 탑승하기
(On the Airplane in Turkey)

Chapter **11**

- 영화 '007 Skyfall' 관광

1. 대화(Target Language)

　비행기가 이륙한 후 몇 분이 지나면 승무원들이 음료 서비스를 시작한다. 그럴 때 사용하는 영어 표현들을 익혀보자.

Would you care for a drink?

What kind of beverages do you have?

I'd like to have coffee.

Would you like chicken of beef?

Beef, please or chicken please.

No Thank you.

옆 사람에게 창문 가림막 좀 내려달라고 부탁할 때

Could you pull the shade down?

비행기가 흔들릴 때

Could you return to you seat, please?

I'm Sorry, but I spilled some coffee.

비행기 도착시간을 물어볼 때

Are we going to arrive on time?

How long will this flight be delayed?

What time do we arrive in san Francisco?

승무원의 영어 표현

We'll arrive at 11:00 local time.

기내에서 속이 불편하거나 토할 것 같은 증세가 있을 때

I feel sick.

I'm not feeling well.

I feel nauseated.

I feel a headache.

Do you have any aspirin?

It's probably airsickness.

Can I have some medicine for nausea?

Excuse me, but do you have medicine for a stomachache?

승무원의 영어 표현

I'll bring you some medicine.

🎞 영화 '007 Skyfall' 관광

　M의 과거에 얽힌 비밀, 거대한 적의 공격으로 위기에 빠진 MI6 제임스 본드, 사상 최강의 적과 맞서라! 상관 M의 지시에 따라 현장 요원 이브와 함께 임무를 수행하던 제임스 본드는 달리는 열차 위에서 적과 치열한 결투를 벌이다 M의 명령으로 이브가 쏜 총에 맞고 추락하여 실종된다. 이에 임무가 실패로 끝나자 전 세계에서 테러단체에 잠입해 임무를 수행 중이던 비밀 요원들의 정보가 분실되고 MI6은 사상 최대의 위기에 빠진다.

　설상가상으로 M의 과거에 얽힌 비밀로 인해 미스터리한 적 '실바'에게 공격을 받은 MI6은 붕괴 위험에 처하게 되고, 이 사건으로 인해 M은 책임 추궁을 당하며 퇴출 위기에 놓인다. 이때, 죽음의 고비에서 부활한 제임스 본드가 M의 곁으로 다시 돌아온다. 절체절명의 위기에 놓인 MI6과 M을 구하기 위해 제임스 본드는 비밀스러운 여인 세버린을 통해 '실바'를 찾아간다. 그리고 마침내 사상 최강의 적 '실바'와 피할 수 없는 대결을 시작하게 되는데…

Asking for Directions

Could you tell me how to get to the Istanbul Biennial?

Excuse me! How do I get to Sultanahmet?

Pardon me, I'm lost. Where is the nearest airport from here?

영화 속 대화

M : Is this where you grew up?

James Bond : Mm.

M : How old were you when they died?

James Bond : You know the answer to that. You know the whole story.

M : Orphans always make the best recruits.

Below is the passage that was quoted. It's taken from Tennyson's Ulysses, which the poet famously claimed described his own "need of going forward and braving the struggle of life" after his friend Hallam's death. It's a very fitting choice for the circumstances in the film, and as Poet Laureate during much of Queen Victoria's reign, he's a very patriotic choice.

The Tennyson quote read by M goes....

> Tho' much is taken, much abides; and though
> We are not now that strength which in old days
> Moved earth and heaven; that which we are, we are;
> One equal temper of heroic hearts,
> Made weak by time and fate, but strong in will
> To strive, to seek, to find, and not to yield.

2. 이스탄불(Istanbul) 소개

Istanbul was the center of Western Civilization for hundreds of years, the center of the Ottoman Empire for hundreds of years, and is today a beautiful water-side city of nearly 15 million energetic people.

Istanbul is a sprawling collection of villages, all of which have exploded into each other, rather than one coherent city. Unless you have months on the ground, you will have to pick one or two Istanbuls and leave the rest for a future trip. Are you interested in slugging it out with the postcard photographers for conventional tourism images of the historic district? Stay in Sultanahmet.

Interested in exploring the relationship among the city, the two seas, and the strait between the seas? Rent a boat and live on it. Interested in showing the lifestyle of the latest generation of wealthy Turks? Hang out in nightclubs along the Bosphorus. Interested in how people from poor villages in the southeast adapt to the cost and secular life of the big city? Visit the slums and the factories.

1) Istanbul Bazaar : The Religion of Shopping

A lot of folks would suggest starting a tourist or photographic project in Istanbul in the mosques. In Istanbul, however, urged on by some of the highest living costs in the world, the citizens seem to spend more time thinking about commerce. Why not start in the Bazaar, the world's oldest shopping mall? It is right in Sultanahmet, probably walking distance from your hotel.

Unless you feel like paying more than you'd pay in the U.S., try not to buy anything. If you fall in love with a carpet and don't mind the fact that you could have bought it cheaper in the U.S., any shop can roll it up to be checked through on your flight.

The merchants will tell you that a handmade carpet is a duty-free "handicraft". U.S. customs officials will tell you that a handmade carpet is a carpet and cheerfully collect duty when you arrive back in the States. Don't buy a carpet anywhere that a guide has taken you; the shop will be paying the guide and his company a 40-percent commission.

A reputable shop that does not pay commissions to guides is Sengor Carpet (pronounced "Shangor"; say that "a friend of Oya's sent you").

2) Religion Other than Shopping

Mosques are among Turkey's greatest architectural achievements and Western audiences are very curious to see images relating to Islam. Of all of the cities in Turkey, however, Istanbul is the one where Islam plays the least important role in daily life.

Keeping dogs as family companions and drinking alcohol, both forbidden in most interpretations of the Koran, are more common than daily attendance at the mosque. It is thus somewhat misleading to concentrate your photographic efforts on covered women and people praying.

The most interesting mosques are in Sultanahmet. A non-obvious and not-too-easy-to-find one is Rustem Pasa, up some stairs from a busy nest of market alleys. Rustem Pasa is famous for its ceramic tiles.

3) Tourists

Taking pictures for a glossy souvenir book? Wake up at 6:00 and visit sights before anyone else shows up. Later in the day, wait for fat ugly tourists clad in clashing colors to walk out of the frame. Is that Istanbul as you experienced it? As anyone else is likely to experience it? Tourism has been a feature of the city for centuries. Why not show the sights as they are typically experienced, packed with tourists?

4) Natives

Istanbullus are accustomed to all of the indignities of big city life, including being stared at and photographed by tourists. Try to be quick in raising the camera to your eye and give the subject a big smile as you set the camera back down on your chest.

5) A Higher Perspective

There are no standard airplane or helicopter tours over Istanbul. The easiest way to get above the older areas of downtown is an elevator ride up to the top of the Galata Tower. You'll be looking south towards Sultanahmet, so visit near sunset for the best images. The tower is open until midnight.

6) The Water

Istanbul and environs were built along the Bosphorus, the Golden Horn, the Sea of Marmara, and the Black Sea. For photos of the city from the water, start with the ferry system from Eminonu. Almost any ferry will do, but the system also runs a daily sightseeing round-trip tour.

7) Art Museums and Galleries

The Istanbul Biennial offers the best chance to get interesting photos inside galleries. The Biennial is held every odd-numbered year, i.e., the same years as the Venice Biennale. The Biennial features contemporary art from a variety of countries.

The art tends to be unusual and to occupy large spaces so a photographer is not simply copying paintings. Photography within the exhibits was allowed in 2007. The Istanbul Modern museum is a good starting point for seeing the best

Turkish photography.

8) Side Trip : Cappadocia

The most bizarre built environment in Turkey is Cappadocia, just a one-hour flight to the southeast. The volcanic tuff on the surface facilitated the carving of churches, monasteries, houses, and hotels into rocks. Erosion results in Bryce Canyon-style hoodoos sticking up in the middle of towns. In the bad old days when Mongol and Muslim invaders rode across the plain, the Christians here defended themselves by building massive underground shelters, up to eight levels deep and capable of holding thousands of people.

Cappadocia supports a massive hot air balloon industry, with 28 tourists filling each basket and as many as 50 balloons launching on a typical morning. I rode with Cihangir Balloons, piloted by Cihangir, a rock solid guy with 4000 airplane hours who turned to balloons 15 years ago.

Highly recommended. Earplugs are essential, at least for the one ear closest to the burner. Layers are also a good idea as it starts out cold (pre-sunrise) and ends fairly hot due to burner. You might find it helpful to read our aerial photography tutorial before embarking.

9) Side Trip : Troy

Turks will tell you not to go to the ruins of Troy, which are very ruined indeed. "There's almost nothing to see," they point out, suggesting visits to better-preserved Greek and Roman ruins. For those who've enjoyed The Iliad, however, merely looking out over the plains of Troy from the walls of Ilium will will be worth the flight to Turkey. Troy is reached by a 30-minute flight on a regional jet from Istanbul to Canakkale.

No guides are available within the historic site. It is probably best to hire an independent guide, such as Mustafa Askin, before you drive all the way to the entrance gate. He hangs out at the last restaurant on the right. The food at the restaurant isn't bad, either!

It only takes about one hour to walk around the ruins and read the signs on the self-guided tour.

10) Skip the Dolmabahce Palace

In the 19th Century, the Sultans decided to build themselves a European-style house : the Dolmabahce Palace. The location along the Bosphorus cannot be faulted, but the interior is in hideously bad taste. Some of the materials are luxurious, but mostly the place is an illustration of how many terrible oil painters there were back in the good old days.

Even the most curmudgeon traditionalist will be sold on Abstract Expressionism after a visit to the Dolmabahce Palace. Versailles it ain't. In case you want to see what you're missing by skipping this staple of the bus tours, here are some photos.

11) Shopping Malls

There are a lot of rich people in Istanbul and they love to shop. To get the authentic Turkish shopping experience, don't go to the Bazaar; go to the mall. Kanyon is the most interesting architecturally. The prices probably won't tempt you to buy too much : $7 for an ice cream cone; $250 for running shoes; $1,000 for a pair of high heel shoes; $10,000 for a dress. The identical product can usually be obtained in the U.S. for about half of what it costs here. Due to decades of attacks by Kurds, cars are carefully screened for bombs before being allowed into the parking garages.

12) Hotels

One good hotel that we inspected, not found in any guidebook, is Hotel Sultan Hill. The building is a converted Ottoman-era house, which means that most of the rooms have windows on two sides and therefore much better light than a typical hotel room. The rooms were small but very clean and there is a beautiful roof terrace. The price was 70 Euro for a double, 50 Euro for a single, including breakfast. www.hotelsultanhill.com

13) The Turkish Bath

All of the Turks with whom we spoke reacted with horror when we expressed interest in going to a Turkish Bath (hamam) : "You'll come out dirtier than when you went in"; "They are for poor travelers to the city"; "A 200 lb. hairy Turkish guy will scrub you raw"; "Anyone with money who wants a Turkish bath has one built in his house." None had been to a public hamam at any time during their lives (ranging from 40 to 80 years old).

A friend's uncle told us about a "hotel hamam" that would be clean and, more importantly, staffed with lithe Russian beauties. "It is out near the airport in the Polat Renaissance Hotel. They also have a nice gym."

If they leave their office at 6 the traffic is so bad that they might not get here until 8. People therefore usually stay downtown until 7 and make it here by 8:15 or 8:30. "What does it cost to be a member of such a nice gym? $300 per month (Turkish bath plus exercise for a day tourist was $120). What about salaries at her company, a clothing manufacturer downtown? The seamstresses get paid about $550 per month.

14) Restaurants

Food is excellent throughout Turkey and you are unlikely to be disappointed. Menus tend to be more limited than in the U.S., however, with restaurants concentrating on serving whatever has recently come into season.

Turks love Turkish food and have a tough time imagining why anyone would want to eat anything else. You'll find the ubiquitous pasta and pizza on menus in tourist areas, but otherwise a dearth of international choices.

Bakeries sell quick and inexpensive snacks such as spinach or meat baked into bread. Good luck figuring out how to ask for what you want, though!

The best news for gourmets is that McDonald's is well-established throughout Turkey. The second best news is that Turkey is amply supplied with Haribo

Tropifruit gummi candies.

Internet cafes are common, but typing on a Turkish keyboard is difficult because the English "i" key is in a different place as are many other important characters.

Money is the lira, but merchants often accept the euro and dollar as well. You can get lira with an American ATM card from just about any bank machine. Expect prices for most things to be between 1.2 and 2X the price that you would pay in a large American city.

3. 상황별 대화(Conversation by Situation)

On the Plane 1 : 기내에서 춥거나 음료가 필요한 경우 승무원과의 대화

You	:	Could I get another blanket please? I'm a little cold.
Flight Attendant	:	Certainly, Sir. Would you like a pillow as well?
You	:	No, thanks. But could you please bring me a Coke?
Flight Attendant	:	Sure, would you like ice in that?
You	:	Yes, please.... Oh! Could you also lend me a pen to fill out this immigration form?
Flight Attendant	:	I don't have one on me right now, but I'll get one for you.

(The Flight Attendant Comes Back with Your Drink and a Pen)

You	:	Thanks. Do you know when we will we be landing?
Flight Attendant	:	In about 2 hours.
You	:	What's the temperature in Seattle right now?
Flight Attendant	:	I'm not sure.... I'll check with the pilot.

On the Plane 2 : 좌석을 변경하고 싶어 승무원에게 문의하는 상황

You	: Excuse me, would it be possible to switch/change seats with someone? My wife and I would like to sit together.
Flight Attendant	: Certainly, Sir. For now, please take your seat, and once the plane takes off, I'll help you with that.
You	: Thank you. Could you help me put this bag in the overhead compartment?
Flight Attendant	: Sure... there you go.

(You See that Someone Is Sitting in Your Seat)

You	: I'm sorry, I think you're in my seat sitting wrong.
Other Passenger	: Oh, let me check my boarding pass. Yes, I'm sorry, my mistake.
You	: No problem. I'm going to move anyway. My wife and I would like to sit together.
Other Passenger	: Oh, well, I can switch places with your wife. That way you two can sit together.
You	: Really? That would be great! Thanks a lot.
On the Plane	: What's wrong?

Quiz

다음 대화에서 빈 칸에 들어갈 올바른 단어나 구는?

1. You : Yes, please... Oh! Could you also lend me a pen to _____ this immigration form?

   ① write   ② fill out   ③ make

   Flight Attendant : I don't have one on me right now, but I'll get one for you.

2. (The Flight Attendant Comes Back with Your Drink and a Pen)
   You : Thanks. Do you know when we will be _____?

   ① landing   ② on land   ③ grounding

   Flight Attendant : In about 2 hours.

3. You : I'm sorry, I think you're _____ sitting wrong.

   ① a mistake   ② in my seat   ③ mistake

4. Other Passenger : Oh, let me check my boarding _____. Yes, I'm sorry, my mistake.

   ① pass   ② passport   ③ document

5. You : No problem. I'm going to _____ anyway. My wife and I would
like to sit together.

① transfer   ② move   ③ trade

 ## Vocabulary

1. sick = ill
2. nauseate = disgust, make somebody uncomfortable and sick
3. headache = pain in head
4. stomachache = pain in stomach

Answers

1. fill out   2. landing   3. a mistake
4. pass   5. move

중국에서 운전하기
(Driving in China)

Chapter **12**

- 영화 'The Great Wall' 관광

1. 대화(Target Language)

 여행을 위한 교통수단에는 여러 가지가 있지만 자가용 여행은 여행지의 고속도로, 도심 그리고 지방도로 구석구석까지 속살을 깊이 볼 수 있다는 장점이 있다. 중국의 경우 2007년 이후 '입출경 관리방안'을 개정하여 한국 관광객이 배편으로 차량을 중국에 반입한 뒤 곧바로 운행할 수 있도록 하는 원스톱 서비스를 도입 실시하고 있다. 중국에서 자동차로 여행하면서 웨이하이의 국제해수욕장에서 물놀이를 즐기고 칭다오에 들러 맥주를 한잔 마시는 자동차 여행이 가능하다. 2003년 이후 중국을 통과하여 유럽으로 자동차 여행을 가는 인구수는 점차 증가하고 있으며 최근에는 자동차 여행이 비용을 훨씬 절약할 수 있다는 장점 때문에 젊은 층에서 좋은 호응을 얻고 있다. 유명

관광지가 아니라 시골 곳곳을 누비며 모든 문제를 스스로 해결해야 하기에 주유를 하고 길을 물어보는 등 관련 표현 연습이 절대적으로 필요하다.

Gas Station Attendant	: What can I do for you.
You	: Fill it up, please.... Hey, how far is Shanghai from here?
Gas Station Attendant	: It's about 200 km from here.
You	: What's the best way to get there?
Gas Station Attendant	: Take the 88. That will take you all the way to Shanghai.
You	: Thanks. Is the 88 a toll highway?
Gas Station Attendant	: No, it's free. Would you like me to clean your windshield?
You	: Yes, please.... And could you check my oil as well?
Gas Station Attendant	: All right.... All done. That'll be ￥200.
You	: Here you go. Keep the change.

🎞 The Great Wall

Asking for Directions

How do I find the Forbidden City?

Could you tell me how to get to Yangtze River?

What's the best way to get to Terra Cotta Warriors?

영화 속 대사

Man: I was born in the battle.

I fought for greed and Gods.

This is the first war I've seen, worth fighting for...

2. 중국(China) 소개

China is rich in tourist attractions. The nature has endowed it with spectacular views. The 5,000 years long history has left it with many places of interest. The 56 ethnic groups make the country's folk customs so colorful. Due to all of these, plus unique music, drama and world-known delicacy, China attracts large crowds of tourists from home and abroad every year. China's tourist resources can be primarily divided into three parts : natural landscape, manmade attractions and folk customs.

China boasts a large number of wonderful tour destinations including antique sites and relics, imposing imperial palaces, delicate water towns, amazing natural wonders, splendid cultural heritage, and diversified folk customs. It will take years to visit all of these attractions, but it is fairly easily to tour the top attractions.

Over years, Travel ChinaGuide.com has handpicked many tour itineraries to cover these highlights throughout the country. The well-known Great Wall, Forbidden

City, Summer Palace and Temple of Heaven depict the long and colorful history of Beijing.

The waning residential Beijing Hutongs have transformed into pedestrian streets with trendy shops and bars. Shanghai has become a worldwide metropolis in the last fifty years during last century. From the Bund along the Huangpu River, you can see the city's rapid development, demonstrated by the great changes of the skyline on the Pudong side.

Xian is the shining pearl on the Yellow River along which the ancient Chinese culture originated. The astonishing Terracotta Warriors and Horses of Emperor Qin Shi Huang were excavated in this city and the famous Silk Road started here via brilliant Dunhuang to Europe thousands of years ago.

Winding through eleven provinces and cities, the Yangtze River is the longest river in China. A Yangtze River cruise from Chongqing to Yichang will be an enjoyable holiday with endless green mountains. Comparatively, the picturesque Li River in Guilin is calmer, and the beautiful West Lake in Hangzhou is well cultivated, which is appealing to nature lovers.

Various folk customs and landscapes also formed along these rivers. The cradle of the Yangtze River is on the mysterious Qinghai-Tibet Plateau where you could see the holy Potala Palace, snow-capped Mt. Everest and heavenly Namtso Lake.

When the river reaches the lower Sichuan Basin, there are cute giant pandas and multicolored water of the Jiuzhai Valley waiting for you. The Yellow Mountain situated at the lower reaches of the Yangtze River was included in the UNESCO's World Cultural and Natural Heritage Site List in 1990.

1) Tourism in China

With the sustainable growth of China's economy, the further implementation of the Reform and Opening-up Policy, as well as the substantial increase in its people's personal income, tourism industry of the country has seen unprecedented development in recent years. The enormous outbound market has drawn the attention of the world. The domestic market keeps expanding steadily. However, the inbound market is in a downturn.

2) Inbound Tourism

According to the authority, the total number of overseas tourists had been overall declining slightly after the year 2007. Here are some possible reasons. First, due to RMB appreciation and the fluctuation of the exchange rate, the cost for travel to China goes up, and many potential visitors are thus turning to other destinations.

Second, the economic recession in European and American countries leads people to spend less money in traveling while European and American guests contribute a large proportion to the country's inbound market.

Third, the traditional travel itineraries and products lack novelty and competitiveness. Fourth, compared with other countries, Chinese authorities invest less effort in promoting inbound travel products. Fifth, the decline of the country's national image caused by corruption and other factors has had an adverse impact on inbound market.

And last but not least, air pollution and food security problems arising in recent years cause some foreign visitors to worry about the travel conditions and cancel their plans for China.

Inbound Tourist Arrivals and Growth Rate

출처: TravelChinaGuide.com

3) Folk Customs

China is a big family of 56 ethnic groups, each of whom differs in traditional culture and life styles. For example, Dai People, mainly living in Xishuangbanna of Yunnan, hold Water-Splashing Festival each year.

On this day, people will chase and splash water on each other as they think water is the symbol of luck and happiness. Nadam Fair is Mongolian's annual pageant which is held between July and August.

On this important festival, sport activities such as horse racing, wrestling, tug-of-war and ball games are held, attracting many local people to take part in and visitors to watch. Participate in these colorful activities, and you will learn more about the country's diversified culture.

4) Manmade Attractions

The long Chinese history and splendid culture have left countless sites of historic interest. The industrious Chinese ancient laboring people had created innumerable world wonders such as Great Wall, Terra Cotta Warriors and

Forbidden City, accompanied by the circulation of many stories and allusions. To understand the splendid Chinese culture, you are suggested visiting places of historical interest.

Generally speaking, the historic relics in China can be classified into three groups : holy place of religious culture, rock paintings and grottos, and famous historical and cultural cities. To see the holy place of religious culture, you will get to know how the three main world's religion as well as Chinese native Taoism developed in the country.

The rock paintings and grottos are the gem and the symbol of Chinese ancient art treasure. China has over 100 historical and cultural cities, many of which have a history of over 1,000 years. Strolling in these cities, you will feel time slowly flowing backwards, and this is perhaps the best way to understand their glorious culture and history.

5) Top 10 Cities to Visit

To save your time and energy and allow the best value for your money, we carefully selected the top ten cities to visit in China and the most popular tour packages, in the hope of guiding international travelers especially first-time visitors to better plan their vacation.

3. 상황별 대화(Conversation by Situation)

Driving 1 : Asking Directions - 차에서 레스토랑으로 가는 길을 물어보는 상황

You : Can you recommend a good restaurant around here?

Hotel Clerk : Hmm... there aren't any restaurants around here....

You : What about in city in the city?

Hotel Clerk : There are a lot of good restaurants in the area of the city called Uptown. If you go to Central Avenue, you'll see about 10 different restaurants, all of which are highly recommendable.

You : Great! How do we get to Central Avenue from here?

Hotel Clerk : When you exit the parking lot, turn left on Main Street. Keep driving for about 10 blocks, and you'll come to Central Avenue. Turn right. The restaurant zone is about 5 blocks from there.

You : So, we have to make a right turn on Central Avenue?

Hotel Clerk : That's correct. Would you like me to draw you a map?

You : No, thanks, I think we'll be fine.

Driving 2 : At the Gas Station - 주유소에서 길을 물어보는 상황

Gas Station Attendant : What can I do for you.

You : Fill it up, please.... Hey, how far is Karlsplatz from here?

Gas Station Attendant : It's about 100 miles from here.

You : What's the best way to get there?

Gas Station Attendant : Take the 95. That will take you all the way to Philadelphia.

You : Thanks. Is the 95 a toll highway?

Gas Station Attendant : No, it's free. Would you like me to clean your windshield

You	:	es, please.... nd could you check my oil as well
Gas Station Attendant	:	ll right.... ll done. That'll be . .
You	:	ere you go. eep the change.

Quiz

다음 대화에서 빈 칸에 들어갈 올바른 단어나 구는?

1. You : Fill it up, please... Hey, _____ is philadelphia from here?

   ① what time　　② how long　　③ how far

   Gas Station Attendant : It's about 200 km from here.

2. You : What's _____ to get there?

   ① the road　　② the best way　　③ the good way

   Gas Station Attendant : Take the 88. That will take you all the way to philadelphia.

3. You : Thanks. Is the 88 a _____ highway?

   ① express　　② paying　　③ toll

   Gas Station Attendant : No, it's free. Would you like me to clean your windshield?

4. You : Yes, please... And could you check my _____ as well?

   ① oil　　② tank　　③ fuel energy

   Gas Station Attendant : All right.... All done. That'll be ￥150

5. You : Here you go. _____.

① keep the change   ② put your pocket   ③ you will get it

 **Vocabulary**

1. change   small money
 . handpicked   엄선한
 . depict   describe, characteri e

Answers

1. how far   . the best way   . toll
 . oil   . eep the change.

2 호텔영어
(English for Hotel Staff)

예약받기 및 체크인과 체크아웃
(Taking Reservations & C/I and C/O)

즐거운 여행을 위해서는 숙박업소를 미리 예약해 두는 것이 필수이다. 요즘 대부분의 게스트들은 온라인 및 SNS를 통해 객실을 사전 예약하는데 사전 예약의 경우 필요한 방의 종류와 가격을 세심히 살펴봐야 한다. 유럽의 경우 국가별 성수기와 비수기가 다르기도 하고 주중, 주말의 요금체계도 다르다. 지역에 따라 주중이 주말보다 비싸기도 하고 주말이 주중보다 비싼 곳도 있다. 또 세계적 체인을 가진 호텔의 경우 더블룸을 사용할 때 1인 사용과 2인 사용 시 가격 차이가 있다는 것도 알아둬야 한다.

객실예약을 받는 클럭은 객실 유형별 예약현황을 잘 알고 있어야 하며 다양한 객실요금을 적용하여 최대한 많은 객실을 판매해야 한다. 항상 밝은 목소리로 수신하며 재방문 고객의 경우 목소리를 빨리 인지하여 반갑게 맞이하는 태도를 보이며 객실과 연계한 호텔상품을 추천하여 투숙객이 호텔을 이용하는 동안 즐겁고 유익한 시간이 되도록 최대한 돕는다.

전화벨이 울리면, "Emerald Hotels, Tina speaking. How can I help you?"라고 응대하며 호텔에 도착하는 날짜, 기간, 인원에 대해 파악하는데 기간은 day가 아니라 night 수로 계산해야 한다. 특히 주말이나 연휴로 이어지는 경우는 특별히 유의하여 갑자기 객실이 모자라서 컴플레인이 발생하지 않도록 유의해야겠다.

hat date are you looking for

How long will you be staying?

How many adults will be in the room?

더 이상 빈 객실이 없을 경우/혹은 극히 소수가 남은 경우

I'm afraid we are booked that weekend.

There are only a few vacancies left.

We advise that you book in advance during peak season.

객실 유형에 관한 안내를 할 때

Will two double beds be enough?

Do you want a smoking or non-smoking room?

객실요금에 대한 안내

The rate I can give you is $176 with tax.

We require a credit card number for a deposit.

호텔 내 부대시설 이용에 관한 정보 안내

The dining room is open from 4 pm until 10 pm.

We have an indoor swimming pool and sauna.

We serve a continental breakfast.

Cable television is included, but the movie channel is extra.

자동차를 이용하여 호텔로 오고 있는 고객에게 길을 안내할 때

Take Exit 8 off the highway and you'll see us a few kilometers up on the left hand side.

Guest

고객이 예약상황, 추가침대 및 베이비코트 사용 시 추가요금 그리고 객실요금에 조식이 무료로 포함되는지에 관해 문의한다.

I'd like to make a reservation for next week.
Is it necessary to book ahead?
Do you charge extra for two beds?
How much is it for a cot?
Do you offer free breakfast?

좀 더 가격이 낮은 객실이 있나요?
Do you have any cheaper rooms?

비수기는 언제인가요?
When is it considered off-season?

단체예약도 받나요?
Do you do group bookings?

야외 수영장이 있나요?
Is there an outdoor pool?

호텔 내에 레스토랑이 있나요?
Is there a restaurant in the hotel?

객실 내에 냉장고가 있나요?
Do the rooms have refrigerators?

Sample Conversation

Receptionist : Thanks for calling Quality Inn. Morine speaking.

Caller : Hello. I'm interested in booking a room for the September long weekend.

Receptionist : I'm afraid we're totally booked for that weekend. There's a convention in town and we're the closest hotel to the convention centre.

Caller : Oh, I didn't realize. Well what about the weekend after that?

Receptionist : So.... Friday the seventeenth?

Caller : Yes. Friday and Saturday.

Receptionist : It looks like we have a few vacancies left. We recommend that you make a reservation, though. It's still considered peak season then.

Caller : Okay. Do you have any rooms with two double beds? We're a family of four.

Receptionist : Yes, all of our rooms have two double beds. The rate for that weekend is $129 dollars a night.

Caller : That's reasonable. And do you have cots? One of my daughters might be bringing a friend.

Receptionist : We do, but we also charge an extra ten dollars per person for any family with over four people. The cot is free.

Caller : Okay, but I'm not positive if she is coming. Can we pay when we arrive?

Receptionist : Yes, but we do require a fifty dollar credit card deposit to hold the room. You can cancel up to five days in advance and we will refund your deposit.

Caller : Great, I'll call you right back. I have to find my husband's credit card.

Receptionist : Okay. Oh, and just to let you know... our outdoor pool will be closed, but our indoor pool is open.

Check Your Understanding

1. Why did the caller phone this hotel?

   a) to change a reservation

   b) to report a cancellation

   c) to inquire about available rooms

   Tick for answer : c

2. Why can't the caller stay at the hotel on the September long weekend?

   a) The hotel is fully booked.

   b) The hotel has a convention.

   c) The hotel is closed for the season.

   Tick for answer : a

3. Why does the caller have to hang up and call back?

   a) She wants to research other hotels.

   b) She needs to discuss things with her husband.

   c) She needs to find the credit card to pay the deposit.

   Tick for answer : c

Checking Guests In and Out(체크인 때 사용되는 영어 표현들)

호텔에서의 체크인과 체크아웃에 필요한 표현들이다. 반복적인 연습과 문제 풀이로 확실하게 내 것으로 만들도록 하자.

Check In

Front Desk Receptionist

• What name is the reservation under?

• How long will you be staying?

• Are you planning on checking out tomorrow?

• I'm afraid you can't check in until after 4:00 pm.

• What type of vehicle are you driving?

• Do you know the license plate number of your vehicle?

• Complimentary breakfast is served in the lobby between 8 and 10 am.

• I'll give you two room keys.

• The dining room is on the main floor at the end of the hall.

• The weight room and sauna are on the top floor.

• Just call the front desk if you need any extra towels or pillows.

Guest

• We have a reservation under Jill McMann.

• Do you have any vacancies?

• Is the hotel booked, or can we get a room for tonight?

• How do we get to our room from here?

• Is it okay to park out front?

• What time is the pool open until?

• What time is breakfast served at?

• Is it too early to check in?

• Can we get a wake-up call?

• When is check out time?

Check Out

Front Desk Receptionist

- Are you ready to check out?
- What room were you in?
- How was your stay?
- Was everything satisfactory?
- Will you be putting this on your card?
- And how will you be paying for this?
- Would you like to speak to the hotel manager on duty?
- I'll just need your room keys, please.
- Enjoy the rest of your holiday.
- Have a safe trip home.

Guest

- We're checking out of room 401.
- Sorry we're a bit late checking out.
- I'm afraid we overslept/slept in.
- We really enjoyed our stay.
- We have a few complaints.
- We'll be back next time we're in town.

Sample Conversation(샘플 대화)

Receptionist : Hi there. Are you checking out now?

Guest : Yes, sorry. I know we're a few minutes late.

Receptionist : That's no problem. It's always really busy at check out time anyway.

Guest : Oh, really. The last hotel we stayed in charged us for a late check out.

Receptionist : The hotel isn't booked this week, so it's not a problem. How was everything?

Guest : The room was great. The beds were really comfortable, and we weren't expecting our own fridge.

Receptionist : I'm glad you liked it.

Guest : The kids were disappointed that the pool wasn't open this morning, though.

Receptionist : I apologize for that. We can't get a cleaner in any earlier than 10 am.

Guest : Well we had a nice swim last night anyhow.

Receptionist : Will you be putting this on your credit card?

Guest : No. I'll pay cash.

Receptionist : OK. So the total comes to $123.67, including tax.

Guest : I thought it was $115 even. That's what they said yesterday when we checked in.

Receptionist : Yes, but there is an extra room charge on your bill.

Guest : Oh, I forgot. My husband ordered a plate of nachos. Sorry.

Receptionist : No problem. So... from $140, here's your change. Now, I'll just need to ask you for your room keys.

Test Your Understanding

1. Why does the guest apologize when she arrives at the front desk?

    a) She forgot to pay.

    b) She is late checking out.

    c) Her credit card isn't working.

    Tick for answer : b

2. Which of the following did the woman's family not like about the hotel?

    a) the pool hours

    b) the room rates

    c) the bed clothing

    Tick for answer : a

3. What was the woman charged for besides the room rate?

    a) telephone use

    b) room service

    c) pool towels

    Tick for answer : b

호텔용어(Hotel Vocabulary)

다음은 호텔은 물론 다양한 숙박업체에서 국제적으로 통용되는 전문용어들이다. 단어와 구를 포함하여 제시된 문장을 보고 이를 응용하여 새로운 문장을 작성하고 말하기 훈련의 반복을 통해 자다가도 퍼뜩 머리에 떠오를 수 있도록 외워둔다. 이어지는 팝 퀴즈를 통해 용어들에 대한 이해도를 높이자.

(1) Adjoining Rooms

two hotel rooms with a door in the centre

If you want we can book your parents in an adjoining room.

: _____

(2) Amenities

local facilities such as stores and restaurants

We are located downtown, so we are close to all of the amenities.

: _____

(3) Attractions

things for tourists to see and do

The zoo is our city's most popular attraction for kids.

: _____

(4) Baggage

bags and suitcases packed with personal belongings

If you need help with your baggage we have a cart you can use.

: _____

(5) Bed and Breakfast

a home that offers a place to stay and a place to eat

I can book you into a beautiful Bed and Breakfast on the lake.

: _____

(6) Bellboy

a staff member who helps guests with their luggage

The bellboy will take your bags to your room for you.

: _____

(7) Book

arrange to stay in a hotel

I can book your family in for the weekend of the seventh.

: _____

(8) Booked

full, no vacancies

I'm afraid the hotel is booked tonight.

: _____

(9) Brochures

small booklets that provide information on the local sites and attractions

Feel free to take some brochures to your room to look at.

: _____

(10) Check-In

go to the front desk to receive keys

You can check-in anytime after four o'clock.

: _____

(11) Check-Out

return the keys and pay for the bill

Please return your parking pass when you check-out.

: _____

(12) Complimentary Breakfast

free of charge

All of our rooms have complimentary soap, shampoo, and coffee.

: _____

(13) Cot, Rollaway Bed

a single bed on wheels that folds up

If you need an extra bed, we have cots available.

: _____

(14) Damage Charge

money a guest owes for repairs to hotel property (when caused by violent or
careless acts)

We will have to add a damage charge for the hole you put in the wall.

: _____

(15) Deposit

amount paid ahead of time to secure a reservation

You will not receive your deposit back if you cancel.

: _____

(16) Double Bed

a bed large enough for two people

They are a family of four, so give them a room with two double beds.

: _____

(17) Floor

a level of the building

The swimming pool is on the main floor.

: _____

(18) Front Desk, Reception

the place where guests go to check in and out and to get information

Towels are available at the front desk.

: _____

(19) Guest

a person that is staying at the hotel

Our washrooms are for guests only.

: _____

(20) Hostel

a very inexpensive place for backbackers and travelers on a budget

In the hostel you probably won't get your own room.

: _____

(21) Hotel Manager

person in charge at the hotel

I'll let you make your complaint to the hotel manager.

: _____

(22) Housekeeping, Maid Noun

staff members that clean the rooms and linen

Put a sign on the door if you want housekeeping to come in and change the sheets on the bed.

: _____

(23) Ice Machine

a machine that automatically makes ice that guests can use to keep drinks cold

There is an ice machine by the elevator on all of the even numbered floors.

: _____

(24) Indoor Pool

place for guests to swim inside the hotel

The heated indoor pool is open until 10 pm.

: _____

(25) Inn

another word for "hotel"

There's an inn on the other side of town that has a vacancy.

: _____

(26) Jacuzzi, Hot Tub, Whirl Pool

a small hot pool for relaxation

Our honeymoon room has a personal hot tub.

: _____

(27) King-Size Bed

extra large bed

A room with a king size bed costs an extra ten dollars a night.

: _____

(28) Kitchenette

a small fridge and cooking area

Your room has a kitchenette so you can prepare your own breakfasts and
    lunches.

: _____

(29) Late Charge

a fee for staying past the check-out time

You will be charged a ten dollar late charge for checking out after 11 am.

: _____

(30) Linen

sheets, blankets, pillow cases

We will come in and change the linens while you are out of your room.

: _____

(31) Lobby

   large open area at the front of the hotel

   You can stand in the lobby and wait for your bus.

   : _____

(32) Luggage Cart

   a device on wheels that guests can push their luggage on

   Please return the luggage cart to the lobby when you are finished with it.

   : _____

(33) Maximum Capacity

   the most amount of people allowed

   The maximum capacity in the hot tub is ten people.

   : _____

(34) Motels

   accommodations that are slightly cheaper than hotels

   Our motel is very clean and is close to the beach.

   : _____

(35) Noisy : adj.

   loud

   The guests next to you have complained that you are being too noisy.

   : _____

(36) Parking Pass

   a piece of paper that guests display in the car window while in the hotel
       parking lot

   Display this parking pass in your window to show that you are a hotel guest.

: _____

(37) Pay-Per-View Movie

extra charge for movies and special television features

If you order a pay-per-view movie, the charge will appear on your bill.

: _____

(38) Pillow Case

the covering that goes over a pillow

Room 201 doesn't need their sheets changed, but they requested one new
pillow case.

: _____

(39) Queen Size Bed

bed with plenty of space for two people (bigger than a double)

They have a queen size bed so the small child can easily fit in the middle.

: _____

(40) Rate

cost of renting a room for a certain time period

Our rates change depending on the season.

: _____

(41) Reservation

a request to save a specific room for a future date

They say they made a reservation but it doesn't show on the computer.

: _____

(42) Room Service

delivery of food or other services requested by guests

If you would like a bottle of wine, just call room service.

: _____

(43) Sauna

a hot room for relaxation, filled with steam

We don't recommend bringing young children into the sauna.

: _____

(44) Single Bed

a bed for one person

The economy priced room includes one single bed.

: _____

(45) Sofa Bed, Pull-Out Couch

a bed built into a sofa or couch

The room contains a sofa bed so the room actually sleeps five.

: _____

(46) Towels

used to cover and dry the body after swimming or bathing

You can get your swimming pool towels at the front desk.

: _____

(47) Vacancy

available rooms

We only have one vacancy left, and it is for a single room.

: _____

(48) Valet

staff that parks the guests' vehicles

If you leave your car keys with us, the valet will park your car underground.

: _____

(49) Vending Machine

a machine that distributes snacks and beverages when you insert coins

The vending machine on the fifth floor has chocolate bars and chips.

: _____

(50) View

a window that offers a nice image for guests

The room is more expensive because it has a spectacular view of the beach.

: _____

(51) Wake Up Call

a morning phone call from the front desk, acts as an alarm clock

What time would you like your wake up call?

: _____

(52) Weight Room, Workout Room, Gym

a room that guests can use for exercise and fitness

Our weight room has a stair climber and a stationary bicycle.

: _____

Hotel Vocabulary Quiz

This quiz is based on our hotel vocabulary above.

01. If you've never been to this city, you should take a look at our — a) menu b) brochures c) front desk.

02. Sorry, we don't have a — a) room b) laundry c) valet service. You'll have to park your car yourself.

03. The room has a pull — a) off b) over c) out couch, so it will sleep an extra person.

04. We don't have any vacancies. We are completely — a) vacant b) booked c) closed.

05. After your long conference you can relax in the — a) kitchenette b) parking lot c) hot tub.

06. I'll call housekeeping and ask them to bring you some fresh — a) ice b) milk c) linen.

07. If you need to do your workout we have a — a) weight room b) restaurant c) library on the third floor.

08. I'll let you voice your complaint about the rate to the — a) housekeeper b) valet driver c) hotel manager.

09. Please put your used — a) dishes b) towels c) menus in the basket and leave unused ones hanging on the rack.

10. If you need a midnight snack there's a — a) bellboy b) kitchenette c) vending machine full of potato chips on your floor.

Answer : 1. b / 2. c / 3. c / 4. b / 5. c / 6. c / 7. a / 8. c / 9. b / 10. c

인사와 소개
(Greetings & Introduction)

Chapter **3**

First impressions last a life time, or at least until the guests check out, so it is important to make a good first impression. There are numerous expressions that can be used when first greeting hotel guests. Some are very formal and appropriate for greeting guests and some are more informal and should only be used with friends or co-workers. Obviously, employees of the hotel industry should use the more formal expressions, however the less formal expressions will also be presented to give learners a well balanced repertoire to choose from.

첫 인상이 평생을 간다는 말이 있듯이 호텔은 호스피텔러티 산업의 정점에 있는 직업이다. 호텔에 처음 들어서는 순간의 인상은 오래도록 고객의 마음을 지배하므로 도어맨 및 벨데스크와 프런트 직원들은 항상 최선의 서비스를 제공하는 전문인으로서의 자세를 유지해야 한다.

Formal Expressions

호텔에서는 대부분 각 언어의 극존칭에 가까운 용어를 사용한다.

Good morning (Sir/Ma'am)

Good afternoon (Sir/Ma'am). Welcome to (name of hotel/shop, etc)

Good evening (Sir/Ma'am)

How are you this morning (afternoon, evening, today)?

호텔 현관이나 로비에 들어서는 고객에게 혹은 서성거리는 고객에게는 먼저 다가가서 "무엇을 도와 드릴까요"라고 말을 건넨다.

How can I help you today Ma'am (Sir)?

Can I be of assistance?

How may I assist you?

May I assist you with anything?

What can I do for you today?

Dialogue for Greeting Guests at Spa & Massage(마사지 고객)

Staff　：Good morning Ma'am. Welcome to the Spa & Massage.

Guest　：Thank you.

Staff　：How can I help you today?

Guest　：I'm here for Thai massage.

Expressions for Farewells(고객에게는 "다시 또 오세요."라고 인사)

More Formal Expressions – 격식을 갖춘 인사 표현

Goodbye

Thank you for coming. Have a pleasant day.

Goodbye, please come again.

Goodbye, I hope to see you again.

Less Formal Goodbyes - 격식을 덜 차린 표현

See you later (soon)	So long
Good bye	Bye
I have to run	I have to be going now
Catch you later	Later
See you again	Please come again

Introducing Yourself(고객에게 격식을 갖춰 자신을 소개하는 직원)

Staff : Hello, I'm Ms. Jabdee.

Guest : Hello, Ms. Jandee, I'm Susan Appleton.

Guest : My name is John Grey.

Staff : Nice to meet you Mr. Grey, I'm Mrs. Sukjoy.

Guest : I'm George Franks. What's your name?

Staff : My name is Sopida, Sopida Hakam. It's a pleasure to meet you Mr. Franks.

Guest : Allow me to introduce myself. My name is Frank Jeffers.

Staff : I delighted to meet you Mr. Jeffers. My name is Pornpan Orasa.

투숙객 요청
(Guests Requests)

특급호텔에서 고객은 지불하는 만큼의 서비스를 기대한다. 그러므로 '고객의 요구는 대체로 합리적이다'라는 전제하에 극진한 서비스를 제공할 필요가 있다. 가끔 고객의 부당하다고 생각되는 요구에 잘 대처하지 못해 컴플레인이 발생할 수 있는데 그때는 우선 정중하게 고객의 의견을 경청하고 감정을 배제한 프로다운 자세로 대처한다. 가능하다면 사무실로 모시고 가서 의자에 앉게 한 뒤 물이나 차를 한 잔 권한다면 고객이 격한 감정을 누그러뜨리는 데 많은 도움이 될 것이다.

Expressions Used for Making Requests(다양한 요청을 하는 고객)

Request : Could I have another order of garlic toast?

Response : Yes Sir, I'll take care of that right away.

Request : I would like extra soap and shampoo left in the room.

Response : I'll attend to that immediately.

Requests : Would it be possible to get a two minute boiled egg?

Response : Of course Sir, I'll be back with that item in a few minutes.

Request : Could you arrange a tee time of 7:00 am for four at the Country

Club?

Response : Of course Sir, what is the name of your party.

Requests : The guests in the next room are very noisy. Could we change rooms?

Response : I'm not sure, let me talk to my supervisor. I'll be back in a moment.

Request : Is it possible to get free samples of all the facial products the spa sells?

Response : Certainly ma'am, which products would you like?

Dialogue for Guests Requests(피트니스클럽에서 고객의 요청)

Guest : Instead of herbal tea, do you happen to have Earl Grey?

Staff : I'm sorry ma'am, but herbal tea is all we have at the moment.

Guest : Could I get some more weights added to this machine. This is no challenge at all.

Staff : I'll get more weight right away. How much more?

Guest : Could you fill out the form for me. I hurt my writing hand?

Staff : Of course Sir. First, how do you spell your family name?

불만사항 (Complaints)

호텔은 우리 집에 손님을 맞이한 상황의 확대판이라고 생각하면 된다. 그런데 성수기에 수백 명의 고객이 한꺼번에 객실과 레스토랑, 그 외 부대시설을 이용할 경우 발생하는 컴플레인에 대한 세련된 대처는 평소 교육을 통한 훈련 없이는 이루어질 수 없다. 그러므로 상세한 매뉴얼과 프로 정신에 입각한 컴플레인 처리 능력을 반복 훈련하여 최상의 시설을 갖추고 최상의 서비스를 할 줄 아는 서비스 전문인으로서의 능력을 발휘할 수 있도록 하자.

Expressions Used for Handling Guest's Complaints 1(컴플레인 발생과 대처)

Complaint : There are not enough towels in my room.

Response : I'll have housekeeping deliver more towels to your room right away Sir.

Complaint : The sink is leaking in the bathroom.

Response : Sorry for the inconvenience, maintenance will be by shorty to fix the problem.

Complaint : This tread mill doesn't seem to be working properly.

Response : I'm sorry miss, why don't you used that one over there.

Complaint : I seem to have misplaced my tennis racket. Has one been turned in?

Response : Not yer Sir, but I'll let you know if someone does. What is your room number?

Complaint : I specifically requested an ocean view, but the room I was given has a view of the pool.

Response : I'm sorry about the mix up Sir, we'll change your room immediately.

Complaint : This soup is not warm enough.

Response : I apologize for that ma'am. I'll have the chef warm it up immediately.

Complaint : Why is our order taking so long?

Response : Well Sir, you ordered the steak very well done and it takes a little longer.

Dialogue about Handling Complaint 2(고객의 컴플레인과 대처)

Guest : When I first arrived I was assured that a bottle of Chivas Regis would always be in the mini-bar. Well I'm here now and the bottle isn't. What kind of hotel are you running here anyway!

Staff : I sincerely apologize for the oversight Sir. We have been exceedingly busy today because of the convention. I'll have a complimentary bottle delivered immediately. Please accept it with our compliments.

Guest : Well, I should hope it would be complimentary. Thank you. Good bye.

Guest : This tea is sweetened, and I specifically wanted unsweetened tea.

Staff : I'm sorry ma'am. I'll bring an unsweetened tea immediately. Please excuse the mistake.

Guest : No problem, things happen.

Staff : Here's your tea ma'am. Let me know if I can be of further assistance. Enjoy the rest of your meal.

Guest : Thank you.

Guest : I had reserved a tennis court, but it has been taken over by someone else.

Staff : Yes Sir, I understand. But we have a policy that if a party is more than 15 minutes late for a starting time, we schedule the courts for other waiting guests. I'm so sorry for the inconvenience. Would you like to reschedule?

Guest : I requested the eggs over hard, these are over easy.

Guest : Sorry about that Sir, let me make you some more right away.

Guest : We ran out of toilet paper. Is it possible to get more?

Staff : Of course, ma'am. I'll send more up immediately. Is there any thing else you require?

Guest : Now that you mention it, could you also bring up a six pack of Heineken?

Staff : Yes ma'am, I'll notify room service and have them send some to your room.

Guest : That would be great, thanks.

조언해 주기
(Giving Advice)

여행 중 모든 것이 낯선 곳에서 조언을 구하는 표현들이다. 레스토랑에서 메뉴를 잘 이해할 수 없을 때 종종 웨이터에게 나의 상황을 설명하고 메뉴 선택에 대한 조언을 구하듯이 일상에서도 어떤 선택을 하거나 결정할 때 정중한 표현으로 조언을 구해보자.

Expressions Used for Offering or Giving Advice

When Asking for Advice - 조언을 구하고자 할 때

What do you think I should do?

What would you do in my shoes?

Do you have any ideas about what to do?

What would you suggest?

Can you think of anything that might help?

When Giving Advice - 내가 권유를 하거나 충고해 주고 싶을 때의 완곡한 표현

Why don't you (.... take a taxi instead, it's faster.)

Have you thought about (.... getting some medicine at the pharmacy)?

I think you should (.... see a doctor).

Have you considered (.... the local markets? Sometimes they have great deals).

One option may be to (.... call you embassy).

When Responding to Advice(조언에 대한 반응의 표현)

That's a good idea. That might work. I hadn't thought of that.
Maybe you're right. Thanks for the advice. Thanks, I'll try that.

Dialogue for Giving Advice - 고객에게 완곡하게 조언하는 대화

Guest : That food was really spicy and upset my stomach.

Staff : Maybe you should get some medicine at a pharmacy.

Guest : That's a good idea. Thanks.

Guest : That woman looks angry. Did I do something wrong?

Staff : Actually Sir, that gesture you used is considered very rude in our culture.

Guest : I'm sorry, I didn't mean to offend anyone. What should I do in that situation?

Staff : Using this gesture instead is appropriate.

Guest : Thanks for the advice.

Guest : I can't seem to find any of the souvenirs I want at the mall. I can't go home empty handed. Do you know where I could go?

Staff : Have you considered shopping at the traditional open market. It has hundred of items to chose from and the prices are usually cheaper than in the mall.

Guest : Thanks, I'll try that.

계산서 정산
(Bill Settlement)

호텔에서의 체크아웃은 투숙하는 동안 이용했던 모든 상품에 대한 계산을 하는 것이다. 이에 필요한 여러 가지 표현들을 배워두자.

Expressions Used for Bill Settlement(계산할 때 사용하는 표현들)

How will you be paying?	Do you accept VISA or Master Card?
Could you sign here please?	There you are.
Here's you change Sir.	That's OK, keep the change.
Would you like a receipt?	Could I have a receipt please?
I'll check the bill again if you like.	This seems a bit much.
	Can this be right?
	I think there's been a mistake on the bill.
Let me double check that for you Ma'am.	
	Is a tip or gratuity included in the bill?
Yes, a service charge is included in the bill.	

From Staff X	From Guests
Will that be cash or charge?	I'll be paying with cash.
How will you be paying?	Do you accept VISA or Master Card?
Could you sign here please?	There you are.
Here's you change Sir.	That's OK, keep the chang
Would you like a receipt?	Could I have a receipt please?
I'll check the bill again if you like	This seems a bit much.
Let me double check that for you ma'am.	Can this be right?
Yes, a service charge is included in the bill.	I think there's been a mistake on the bill.
	Is a tip or gratuity included in the bill?

Dialogues for Bill Settlement(계산할 때 고객과의 대화)

Guest : Could I have the check please?

Staff : Of course Sir, I'll be back in a moment.

Guest : I'd like to check out please.

Staff : Of course Sir, could I have your room number and room key?

Guest : The room was 333. Here's the key.

Staff : Did you use the mini bar Sir?

Guest : Yes, I had a couple of sodas.

Staff : The total comes to $577.99. Will you be charging this Sir?

Guest : Yes, put it on my Visa Card.

Staff : Sign here please. And thank you for staying with us.

Guest : There you go. Thanks.

Staff : How will you be settling your bill Sir?

Guest : I'll be paying by cash.

Staff : Yes Sir, here's the bill.

Guest : Excuse me, but what is this charge for?

Staff : Let me see, it's for an apple pie.

Guest : But we didn't order apple pie.

Staff : I'm terrible sorry for the error Sir. Let me refigure this. Here you go Sir.

Guest : That looks right. Thank you.

Staff : Sorry for the error Sir, and please come again.

Staff : Would you like to pay for the tennis court in cash or charge it to your room?

Guest : Just charge it to my room please.

Staff : Yes Sir, if you could just sign here.

Guest : There you are.

Staff : Thank you Sir, have a pleasant day.

Whole Class Activity - Vocabulary : First to Know - 꼭 알아둬야 할 용어

전문용어의 뜻을 영어로 말할 수 있도록 외우고 반복하여 소리내어 읽는다. 영어회화할 때 훨씬 폭넓고 자연스럽게 말하고자 하는 의미를 전달할 수 있게 된다.

Supplement : An addition to something

Amount : The cost of something

Sub-total : The amount of part of a bill

Total : The entire cost of something

Exchange Rate : The cost of one currency compared to another

Room Rate : The price of a room at a hotel

Charge : To pay for something with a credit card

Discount : An amount subtracted from the total

Invoice : Another word for bill

Coupon	:	A paper with a set price (usually discounted) for a good
Balance	:	The amount of money remaining (usually in a bank account)
Debit	:	To subtract from a balance
Credit	:	To add to a balance
Deposit	:	To put money into a bank account
Gratuity	:	An extra amount added to a bill given to a waiter or waitress for good service
Tip	:	A gratuity
Service charge	:	An additional amount added to a bill
Tax	:	An amount added to a bill that goes to the government

호텔 부대시설
(Facilities/Amenities)

Chapter **8**

대부분의 호텔은 게스트들이 머무는 동안 즐거운 시간을 가질 수 있도록 부대시설을 갖추고 있다. 호텔 시설로 비즈니스센터는 물론 실내·외 수영장, 사우나, 찜질방, 피트니스센터, 테니스코트, 다양한 레스토랑 그리고 야외공연장, 기타 공연장 외 독특한 클럽들을 갖춘 호텔도 있다. 호텔은 단순히 숙박만 제공하는 곳이 아니라 세련된 시설과 표준화된 서비스로 고객 개개인의 요구에 부응하는 것을 지향하고 독특하고 개성 있는 건축디자인과 인테리어, 운영 콘셉트, 서비스 등으로 차별화를 추구한다. 또한 특급호텔들은 갤러리를 연상시킬 정도로 진귀한 예술품을 전시하거나 고객 맞춤형 이색 서비스를 제공하기도 하는데 이러한 고급스러운 분위기의 연출로 소수를 위한 틈새시장을 공략한다.

다음은 호텔 내에서 많이 사용되는 관련시설 및 활동에 쓰이는 용어 리스트이니 익혀두도록 하자.

At a Hotel	In the Community
Restaurants	Shopping Malls
Cafés	Scuba Diving
Lounges	Snorkeling
Spas	Golf
Saunas	Island Tours

Steam Rooms	Boat Charters
Gift Shops	Elephant Treks
Gym/Fitness Centers	Zoos
Conference Rooms	Museums
Business Centers	Panoramic Vistas
Swimming Pools	Aquariums
Squash Courts	Sea Kayaking
Tennis Courts	Open Traditional Markets
Putting/Chipping Greens	Nature Treks
Children's Programs	Grocery Stores

Dialogue about Hotel Facilities and Amenities(호텔의 부대시설 이용을 위해 문의하는 고객과의 대화)

Guest : We're looking for a good restaurant for dinner?

Staff : What kind of food are you interested in?

Guest : Since we are in Thailand, we want to try Thai food.

Staff : The Thai Restaurant is always a good choice.

Guest : Thank you very much. We'll try it.

Guest : Could you recommend a place to take our kids? They're getting bored at the beach.

Staff : There's a movie theater in Phuket Town at Central Festival they might enjoy.

Guest : Well maybe. Is there anything else more exciting?

Staff : Lots of kids seem to have a great time at the Go-Cart track.

Guest : No way. That's way too dangerous.

Staff : Have they ever ridden an elephant?

Guest : No, but is it safe?

Staff : Oh, absolutely. The elephants are well trained and the trainer leads the elephant along the path. Riders are strapped into the seats with safety belts, just like in a car. And to be truthful, the rides are not that long- 30 minutes or so.

Guest : That sounds OK.

Guest : I need to check my e-mail. Is there an Internet café near here?

Staff : Certainly, Sir. The Business Center at the hotel has Internet access.

Guest : Can I also surf the Internet there? I need to find some information for a meeting.

Staff : Absolutely Sir.

Guest : Can I also save information to a disk or flash memory?

Staff : Of course.

Guest : Do you know what it cost?

Staff : To be honest Sir, I don't really know. But I'm sure it's a nominal fee.

Guest : Ok, thank you.

Staff : My pleasure, Sir.

호텔 직업
(Hotel Jobs)

호텔은 고객의 1박을 위해서 백 가지 이상의 품목을 준비하고 있는 곳이므로 업무의 종류 또한 다양하다. 부서의 특성에 따라 업무를 맡은 직원들의 업무형태는 항상 표준화되고 상세히 기록되어 있어 사람이 바뀌어 서비스가 달라지는 일이 없어야 한다. 각자의 직업에 대해 질문하는 표현들을 익혀두자.

Expressions Used to Describe Hotel Jobs(직업을 물을 때)

What do you do?

What's your job?

What do you do for a living?

좀 더 상세하게 하는 업무에 대해 물을 때

What are your job duties?

What exactly do you do?

What does your job entail?

Dialogue about Describing Hotel Jobs(업무에 관한 고객과의 대화)

Guest : What do you do?

Staff : I'm a events coordinator for a hotel?

Guest : What exactly does an events coordinator do?

Staff : Well, we arrange and set up all the things needed for a conventions and conferences for various groups. We try to ensure that every thing runs smoothly and efficiently during the event. For example, we schedule rooms, arrange for the set up of any needed equipment required (such as audio-visual equipment, microphones, etc.), and solve problems that may come up.

Guest : That's sounds interesting.

Staff : It has its moments.

Guest : What's your job?

Staff : I'm a chef.

Guest : Are you a head chef?

Staff : Well, I'm the head pastry chef.

Guest : Sounds sweet. Where do you work?

Staff : At the Hilton Arcadia Spa and Resort.

Guest : What do you do for a living?

Staff : I'm employed at a hotel as a bell man.

Guest : So you take people's luggage to their rooms.

Staff : Yes that, but I also arrange things like taxis for guests. One of my most important functions is to be a source of information. I provide a lot of information to guests, such as the kinds of facilities and their location in the hotel, places to eat in the area, and places to go and see on the island.

Guest : Just out of curiosity- do guests tip well?

Staff　:　Some do, some don't.

Job Descriptions(업무 내용 설명)

- Clerk/Receptionist : This person checks people into the hotel.

- Bell Man : This person takes guest bags to their room.

- Tram Driver : This person drives people to/from various places at the hotel

- Cook : This person prepares food in a restaurant.

- Pastry Chef : This person makes bread, cakes, and cookies.

- Waiter/Waitress : This person serves guests food in a restaurant.

- Hostess : This person greets guests and takes them to their table in a restaurant.

- Bartender : This person makes drinks.

- General Manager : This person is the boss.

- Masseuse : This person gives guests massages.

- Maintenance Worker : This person fixes things that need to be repaired.

- Housekeeper : This person keeps the rooms clean.

- Grounds Keeper : This person cuts grass, trims bushes, and water flowers.

- Guest Relations Agent : This person works with VIP guests.

- Health Center Staff : This person assists guests in the gym.

고전적인 관광명언
(Classic Travel Quotes)

Chapter 10

- The journey not the arrival matters.   _ T. S. Eliot

- Ones destination is never a place, but a new way of seeing things.

_ Henry Miller

- Blessed are the curious, for they shall have adventures.   _ Lovelle Drachman

- A traveler without observation is a bird without wings.   _ Saadi

- Two roads diverged in a wood and I took the one less travelled by.

_ Robert Frost

- Travel brings love and power back into your life.   _ Rumi

- Voyage, travel and change of place impart vigor. _ Seneca

- Tourists don't know where they've been, travelers don't know where they're going. _ Paul Theroux

- One way to get the most out of life is to look upon it as an adventure. _ William Feather

- My favorite thing is to go where I've never been. _ Diane Arbus

- As soon as I saw you I knew an adventure was going to happen. _ Winnie the Pooh

- To travel is to take a journey into yourself. _ Danny Kaye

- We are all travelers in the wilderness of this world, and the best we can find in our travels is an honest friend. _ Robert Louis Stevenson

- Life is a great adventure... accept it in such a spirit. _ Theodore Roosevelt

- Not all those who wander are lost. _ J. R. R. Tolkien

- The world is a book, and those who do not travel read only a page. _ St. Augustine

- A journey of a thousand miles begins with a single step. _ Lao-tzu

- All journeys have secret destinations of which the traveler is unaware. _ Martin Buber

- Do not follow where the path may lead. Go instead where there is no path and leave a trail. _ Ralph Waldo Emerson

- You're off to great places! Today is your day! Your mountain is waiting, so... get on your way. _ Dr. Seuss

- To travel is to live. _ Hans Christian Anderson

저자약력

최창현

현재 가톨릭관동대학교 행정학과 교수로 재직 중이다. 관동대학교 관광학부 겸임교수를 역임했으며 뉴욕주립대학교 객원교수, RPI 경영대학원 초빙교수, 한국공공관리학회 편집위원장, 한국조직학회 회장을 역임했다.

1990년 미국 뉴욕주립대학교(록펠러행정대학원)에서 조직 구조, 직무 만족도, 권위주의에 대한 태도와 조직 몰입도의 관계에 대한 경로 분석적 연구로 행정 및 정책학 박사학위를 받았다. *Introducing Public Administration : Made Easy for TOEIC*(2016), 『공무원영어와 TOEIC』(2005) 등 40여 권의 저서와 역서를 집필했다. 논문은 "문화관광경쟁력의 국제 비교분석 : 한국, 대만, 그리고 중국을 중심으로"(2016), "C-P-N-D 생태계와 ICCT"(2014), "국력요소 중, 소프트파워로서의 문화경쟁력 비교분석 연구"(2014) 등 30여 편이 있다.

임선희

현재 경주대학교 관광경영학과 조교수로 재직 중이다. 파라다이스호텔 객실부에서 10년 이상 근무했고 영국 본머쓰 차인호텔에서 1년 이상 식음료부에서 경험을 쌓았다. 영어영문학 학사이며 영국 본머쓰대학에서 국제관광경영학 석사를 마쳤고 경주대학교에서 문화유산 콘텐츠 활성화 방안을 위한 김춘추 스토리텔링 연구로 관광학 박사학위를 받았다. 대한관광경영학과 이사를 역임하였으며 현재 사단법인 경북MICE관광진흥원 원장으로 활동하고 있다.

저자와의
합의하에
인지첩부
생략

영화로 보는 관광·호텔영어

2016년 10월 30일 초판 1쇄 발행
2018년 1월 26일 초판 2쇄 발행

지은이 최창현·임선희
펴낸이 진욱상
펴낸곳 백산출판사
교 정 편집부
본문디자인 편집부
표지디자인 오정은

등 록 1974년 1월 9일 제406-1974-000001호
주 소 경기도 파주시 회동길 370(백산빌딩 3층)
전 화 02-914-1621(代)
팩 스 031-955-9911
이메일 edit@ibaeksan.kr
홈페이지 www.ibaeksan.kr

ISBN 979-11-5763-295-4
값 15,000원